THE BOOK OF SPELLS FOR BEGINNERS

Revealing The History, Secrets & Practices of Spells, Witchcraft, Magick & More

SOFIA VISCONTI

© Copyright 2022 - All rights reserved.

The content contained within this book may not be reproduced, duplicated, or transmitted without direct written permission from the author or the publisher.

Under no circumstances will any blame or legal responsibility be held against the publisher, or author, for any damages, reparation, or monetary loss due to the information contained within this book, either directly or indirectly.

Legal Notice:

This book is copyright protected. It is only for personal use. You cannot amend, distribute, sell, use, quote, or paraphrase any part, or the content within this book, without the consent of the author or publisher.

Disclaimer Notice:

Please note the information contained within this document is for educational and entertainment purposes only. All effort has been executed to present accurate, up-to-date, reliable, complete information. No warranties of any kind are declared or implied. Readers acknowledge that the author is not engaged in the rendering of legal, financial, medical, or professional advice. The content within this book has been derived from various sources. Please consult a licensed professional before attempting any techniques outlined in this book.

By reading this document, the reader agrees that under no circumstances is the author responsible for any losses, direct or indirect, that are incurred as a result of the use of the information contained within this document, including, but not limited to, errors, omissions, or inaccuracies.

SUBSCRIBE TO SOFIA VISCONTI

Greetings!

As a subscriber, you will receive a **Free Gift** + You will be the first to hear about new books, articles and more exclusives **just for you.**

Simply scan the QR code to join.

CONTENTS

INTRODUCTION 1

CHAPTER 1: MAGICK 5
- WITCHCRAFT 6
- ASTROLOGY 17
- NUMEROLOGY 22

CHAPTER 2: MATERIALS 27
- CANDLES 28
- CRYSTALS 35
- HERBS 37
- OTHER ITEMS 43

CHAPTER 3: PREPARATION 46

CHAPTER 4: CONDUCTING THE RITUAL 49

CHAPTER 5: SPELLS 53
- PURIFICATION SPELLS 54
- HEALING SPELLS 55
- PROTECTION SPELLS 56
- LOVE SPELLS 57
- PROSPERITY SPELLS 58
- INVIGORATION SPELLS 59
- DIVINATION SPELLS 60

CHAPTER 6: SPELLCRAFTING 67
- STEP 1: DETERMINING WHAT YOU WANT 67
- STEP 2: GATHERING THE APPROPRIATE MATERIAL 68
- STEP 3: PLANNING OUT THE RITUAL 69
- STEP 4: TESTING A SPELL 69
- STEP 5: SHARING THE SPELL 70

CHAPTER 7: ALTERNATIVE MAGICK 72

DRUIDISM	72
HEKA	80
KOTODAMA	83
MAGEIA AND GOETEIA	87
MESOPOTAMIA ĀŠIPŪTU	90
OBEAH AND VODOU	98
POWWOW	104
SATANISM	110
SEIÐR AND RUNES	117
THELEMA MAGICK	123
WUISM	130
CHAOS MAGIC	135
CONCLUSION	**140**
REFERENCES	**144**
OTHER BOOKS BY SOFIA VISCONTI	**149**

INTRODUCTION

When someone thinks about magic spells, one may be inclined to think of two different things. The first is the wicked witches with boiling cauldrons and flying brooms, cursing those they dislike and causing havoc wherever they go. The second is the wand-wielding (or staff-wielding) wizard who invokes words of power to cast their magic for either good or evil. However, this book isn't about magic spells. It is about *magick* spells.

Unlike fictional magic, magick does not have the power to turn people into frogs or summon fireballs from thin air. Instead, magick and its craft offers a more subtle approach. Spellcasting using magick offers a way to focus on your life and give you power to achieve your goals. This power is practically invisible compared to the theatrical powers of witches and wizards, but unlike them, this power is real.

Some readers at this point may be skeptical of

such claims. Many will claim that magick is just parlor tricks that are on par with illusionists. However, the truth is that magick is a spiritual experience. In order to properly cast spells, the first step is to open yourself up to the possibility that it exists. If you dismiss magick, no spell you cast will work. You need to have faith in yourself and the spell in order to see results. That is the first step you need to realize if you want to cast spells.

Other readers may be asking who is able to tap into magick. The simple answer is anyone. Unlike fictional works, anyone can cast a spell. It doesn't matter what gender or age you are; anyone can cast a spell. That being said, where you are when you cast the spell does matter, both emotionally and physically. Additionally, most spells need more than simple words in order to work. There is a more complex answer to this though, as this book will show the loose nature of magick and its many forms.

This guide exists to help beginners learn about basic spellcasting. However, this book does more than just explain how one can cast spells. It also goes over the history surrounding the exploration of magick and provides a beginning spell to use for practice. This book also goes over common materials used for spellcasting, enabling beginners and just curious users to experiment with creating spells. It also goes over other practices of spellcasting, as this book focuses primarily on a general form of Wicca. That is not to invalidate the other practices. It is simply because Wicca usually describes itself as practicing witchcraft through various means. There are even some Wiccans that adopt practices from other practices with historical roots. This diverse and freeform way of spellcasting is arguably better for a beginner as they can start off where they feel most comfortable. At the same time, if you wish to go for more complicated practices, that is fine as well. This book is merely a guide to the basics and a jumping off point for further research.

Some might be asking what are the benefits of casting spells. The answer depends on what spell you want to cast. Some spells help improve your well-being. Others enhance your focus and foster better reflection on what you want out of life. A few can help cleanse the body and offer protection from vile things. Alternatively, some spells could be used to invoke pain towards someone you dislike, but it is not advised that you do such spells. Those hurt by magick might seek retribution, which can be dangerous depending on how much damage was dealt. Remember, use magick to better yourself, not to tear others down.

CHAPTER 1
Magick

Before we begin planning out our first spell, we first need to understand the nature of magick. Magick comes from the natural elements within our universe, similar to fictional forms of magic. These elements vary from practice to practice, but each source comes from a fundamental part of our universe. Nature has magick found in the plants that grow around the world. Stars and planets have magick within them, making predictions about a person's future. Stones and crystals can be attuned to better harness magic. There is magick in our thoughts and emotions. Even numbers have some magick about them. There is magick everywhere. It just takes time and a bit of effort to harness it.

Once harnessed, magick can be used to influence the world. Not change, not shift, not alter. Influence. Magick cannot work by itself to make the world a better place or make you achieve your goals. It is simply a helping hand, a way to help accomplish your desires. Just like a person helping you out, though, you need to put in effort as well. Some may point to this fact as a reason to believe that magick has no power, which is an incorrect conclusion. It is a subtle force, but a force that will get the job done if you put in just as much effort.

Some might ask where these ideas come from. In truth, these ideas were formed in separate times by different people. Some fuse these ideas together, seeking to connect magick from all sources. Others view these ideas as separate, putting importance on some while discarding others. There is no unified answer on which sources are more powerful or more reliable. However, even if one doubts the validity of a source, one cannot deny there is history behind them. A history that can often be cruel.

Witchcraft

The origins of witchcraft and witches is a complicated one. That is because many cultures around the world have separate ideas of what constitutes a witch, making it hard to pinpoint which witches are the oldest. For Europeans, some may point to the Bible's Book of Samuel, where King Saul sought a witch to summon a prophet to aid him (History.com Editors, 2017). Others claim that honor belongs to Circe from Homer's *Odyssey* who turned men into animals (Purkiss, n.d.). However, across the Atlantic, the Navajo have their own type of witch. The skinwalker was a witch that could disguise themselves as an animal. And Africa has a history of cannibalistic witches who feast on human blood (Lewis & Russell, n.d.). As one can guess, historical witches were often seen as evil people who sought only personal gain.

As time passed, the idea of witches changed, especially for European witches. With the rise of Christianity, the concept of witches strayed away from the biblical verses that portray witches as communers with the dead. Instead, the Christian faith began to view witches as agents of Satan. This was especially emphasized in the book *Malleus Maleficarum* written by Heinrich Kramer. The book asserted that witches were solely evil in nature and that their spells were aided by the Devil. His book helped inspire witch hunts for centuries.

While many reading this may know of the Salem Witch Trials, they weren't the first instance of a witch hunt. Those trials in 1962 were just one of many that happened after the publication of the *Malleus Maleficarum*. In fact, trials like these predated the book by about six decades, with the earliest noticeable witch trials happening in the early 15th century in Valais, a region in modern-day Switzerland. Starting in 1428, these trials took the lives of 367 supposed witches. In stark contrast to the Salem Witch Trials and other witch trials, the majority of the accused were men.

A thing to note is that many of these witch trials were conducted over a span of years, some lasting entire decades before finally dying down. Additionally, while some had a sudden stop in accusations, others slowly died out with small periods of new cases coming in. The motives behind the trials also change from period to period, with some being religious while others were motivated by selfish desires. However, after the Valais Witch Trials, the *Malleus Maleficarum* became part of the tool kit for new witch hunts across Europe.

A few of these witch hunts include:

- The Trier Witch Trials of 1581, taking place in the Holy Roman Empire, were a notable series of trials as they are often considered to be one of the largest witch hunts in history.
- The North Berwick Witch Trials in 1590s

Scotland.
- The Fulda Witch Trials of 1603, where over 200 Germans died after being accused of witchcraft.
- The Pendle Witch Trials of 1612, where the 12 accused were tried in Lancashire, England.
- The Bamberg Witch Trials of 1627, another German witch hunt with a confirmed death toll of 884 victims (Connolly, 2016).
- The Torsåker Witch Trials started around 1668 in Sweden, but reached a climax in 1675. On one day in that year, 71 accused were beheaded and burned.

While European witch hunts have now become their metaphorical counterpart, other cultures still practice the horrible act. People are still being blamed for the misfortunes of others, even if the person in question doesn't believe in magick. Depending on where you are, you could still be accused of being a witch and face mob justice. While the lack of witch trials in the United States and in Europe may seem like a benefit, the solution to that issue was the creation of a new one. In return for no longer being persecuted, fewer people would believe in the power of witches.

Though science is not a replacement for spirituality, many people believe that it is. The truth is, science can't answer everything without being highly immoral or impractical. At the same time though, science that has been researched for years cannot be replaced by spirituality. The rejection of years of scientific research only results in one making a fool of themselves, and it can further damage the reputation of all spiritual beliefs. Science and the belief in the supernatural may clash from time to time, but both can coexist if practiced in certain ways. Even if people may disagree with that point, they can't deny that witchcraft is still being practiced today.

Not all of modern witchcraft is an extension of earlier practices. This is partially due to the fact that what was considered to be "witchcraft" in older eras were actually practiced by people amongst different faiths. Most often these older systems would be named something else, like "Heka" or "Wu," with the majority of them being attached to a religion. Nowadays, witchcraft is most often associated with a singular group: the Wiccans. While some Wiccan covens still practice traditional rituals, the Wiccans as a whole wish to remove the bad connotations often associated with witches.

While the practices and organization of Wiccan groups can be traced to earlier sources, the name "Wicca" was first created by Gerald Brosseau Gardner. Born in 1884, Gardner was raised in Lancashire, England. His first exposure to occultism started when he moved to Malaya (now known as Peninsular Malaysia) as a civil servant for the English. During his time there, he was exposed to rituals and beliefs conducted by the region's Indigenous peoples. Showing keen interest in these subjects, Gardner began to research into them further, even submitting his work to the *Royal Asiatic Society* journal on his findings in regards to early civilizations of Malaysia (*Gardner, Gerald Brousseau*, n.d.).

Gardner returned to England in the 1930s, where he encountered a coven in Highcliffe, England. This opened Gardner's eyes to the European side of mysticism. This sudden interest was dangerous at the time since English law still outlawed the concept of witchcraft, even if many doubted the harm witchcraft could produce. Despite the threat of legal repercussion, Gardner wrote his first book while in England, calling it *High Magic's Aid*. To evade persecution, he published the book under the pen name "Scire" (*Gardner, Gerald, Brousseau*, n.d.). This danger would later be removed following the end of World War II. In the 1950s, England repealed their laws against witchcraft, allowing Gardner to openly publish one of his most famous works, that being *Witchcraft Today* in 1954 (Wigington, 2019a).

Witchcraft Today introduced the word "wica" to a larger audience, a word Gardener had encountered while interacting with the coven at Highcliffe (History.com Editors, 2018b). The book is composed of Gardener's various theories, experiences, and rituals conducted while being with the Highcliffe coven. With this book, Gardener created his own coven, whose practices influence much of Wicca today. By the time of his death in 1964, Gardener's version of Wicca, known as Gardnerian Wicca, had acquired a decent amount of awareness.

It should be said that this was merely the start for the modern Wiccans. Time had passed since then, and there are many different variations of the practice. Even during Gardener's time, Wiccans were changing, as the second "c" wasn't used until the 1960s (History.com Editors, 2018b). One point that never is truly agreed upon is the definition of a witch. What defines a witch can vary from person to person, some using the term politically while others use it spiritually. Witchcraft is a very loose term that could apply to many things, which works well as the history and current practices can vary greatly between covens.

Due to this loose application, the concept of witches has expanded enough that people have classified witches into different groups. While witches aren't exclusively a single type, the use of such terminology can help one define themselves when talking to other spellcasters. The easiest witch terminology to understand comes when discussing the difference between a "Coven Witch" and a "Solitary Witch." Coven witches are witches that form a group and work together to cast spells and practice their craft. Solitary witches are witches that practice their craft alone, though it doesn't exclude them from talking to other witches about it. These two categories are so broad that literally every witch fits into one of these two categories, though nothing is stopping them from being both.

Despite the rise of Wicca, traditional witches still exist who practice the craft with methods rooted in tradition and history. Because traditional witches encompass a vast array of beliefs and practices, it is more likely that a traditional witch would reference the exact belief system they use in their practice instead of simply calling themselves a traditionalist.

Meanwhile, cosmic witches fuse witchcraft with astrology, a topic that will be discussed later. While certain traditional witches may use parts of astrology, cosmic witches base their magick solely on astral bodies. Due to the nature of astrology, some may argue that cosmic witches were one of the most accepted types of witch in a historical context, though that will be looked into more as we explore astrology later on.

Ceremonial witches take the craft very seriously. While all witches have to conduct rituals, ceremonial witches do so in a more intense fashion, doing spells that are very time consuming to conduct properly. It is advised that a beginner should be wary when joining a ceremonial coven due to the rigid nature of the spells.

Unlike the rigid nature of ceremonial witches spells, eclectic witches take a more personal approach to spells. Eclectic witches are witches that basically fuse the components of different witchcrafts together to form a personal one, allowing for a witch to feel more connected with their craft. This book does lean towards that type of witchcraft as well, as this book takes bits and pieces from several different crafts.

Green witches are witches that mostly use the

elements of nature to do their spells. Witches who practice this usually try to get close to nature when doing their spells, such as going outside or growing the very plants they use in their rituals. Green witches try their best to connect with the Earth and the life that sprouts from it.

Elemental witches are similar, but instead they focus on gaining their magick through the use of four or five elements. These elements are water, fire, earth, air, and sometimes spirit, but not always. Their spells try to harness these elements either with direct material from those elements or through a representation of them.

A witch that could be seen as a fusion between green witches and a water-focused elemental witch is called a sea witch. Sea witches share the quality of the green witches in the sense that they too get their spellcrafting materials from nature, though it is more often associated with aquatic or beachside life. Like elemental witches, the sea witch focuses on the element of water and bases a good portion of their craft around it. Sea witches don't neatly fit in either, however, as they exclude the forestry of the green witches and the other elements of the elemental witches.

There are also some types of witches that could be considered odd to some people. Despite the claims that witchcraft must be connected to some deity or spiritual force, secular witches exist to disagree. While not exclusively atheistic, secular witches believe that their practice is not tied to any divine or unholy beings. Their practice is separate from any form of religion, though that doesn't stop the individual witch from believing in one. They simply separate their craft from their faith.

Another type of witch that might be confusing for some is a kitchen witch. While it may seem odd, kitchen witches perform rituals in their home kitchens, usually during the creation of food. They are often known to infuse their dishes with magick, using herbs in a similar way as a green witch. Kitchen witches may also expand their craft to the entire household, though their major place of casting is within the kitchen. Their spells most focus on the food they prepare, with the aim being to enhance both the dish itself and those who consume it.

As one can see, the history of witches is a complex but often tragic one, though today is a much different story. While not everywhere is safe, more people in the modern-day are accepting of the concept of witches, with certain media portraying witches as helpful and kind people. There are still portrayals of wicked spellcasters, but that has hardly stopped the rise, spread, and diversification of witchcraft. There is still some distrust from certain communities about the practice, but it is rarely dangerous to be a witch in the modern-day.

Astrology

A lot of witchcraft focuses on natural elements as the basis of their beliefs. These can include anything from plants to animals, rocks to mountains, moon to stars. Astrology focuses only on the last pair along with other astral bodies such as other planets. The most popular aspect of astrology is the zodiac, though few know the history surrounding it.

Like witchcraft, the zodiac is incredibly old, with the first one being made by the Babylonians back before the B.C. turned into the A.D. The zodiac divides the year into 12 separate parts, each one aligned to a certain constellation. While the constellation is fixed to a certain time of year, astrologists also examine the surrounding region for other astronomical bodies. These bodies include every planet in our solar system, the Sun, and the Moon. Despite the Sun and Moon not being planets, astrologists call all influencing bodies "planets," which can raise some confusion. For the sake of simplicity, "planets" in this section will be referring to the astrologist's definition, not the astronomer's.

Each planet is tied to a certain human quality. This quality is shifted depending on the position of a planet in relation to a person's zodiac. The qualities of each planet are as follows:

- The Sun is tied to a person's sense of self-worth, confidence, and ego. It is also tied to masculinity.
- The Moon influences the more instinctive side of a person, such as dealing with emotions and intuition. It is also tied to femininity.
- Mercury is the main influencer of a person's logical and communicative abilities.
- Venus is connected to love and artistic expression, as well as the attractions created by such things.
- Mars is associated with passion, both in the good ways and the bad ways. While Mars is a symbol of courage, it is also used to symbolize conflict and aggressiveness.
- Jupiter is connected to a person's luck, prosperity, and sense of hope.

- Saturn is connected to strength, discipline, and the need to follow the law.
- Uranus is connected to freedom, individuality, and chaos. In other words, Uranus reflects qualities opposed to Saturn.
- Neptune is seen as the planet that influences one's spirituality and dreams. However, it also represents deception and illusionary thinking.
- Pluto is connected to transformation and the death of the old. It is tied to a person's personal growth.

Each of these planets also rule over one or two zodiac signs. This rulership simply means the planets influence people with those signs more than others. The most important factor though when considering zodiac signs is a person's birth. The zodiac of a person is determined by their date of birth, and the position of the planets in relation to that zodiac may help predict the personality of the person as they grow up. The 12 signs of the zodiac are: Aries, Taurus, Gemini, Cancer, Leo, Virgo, Libra, Scorpius, Sagittarius, Capricorn, Aquarius, and Pisces.

While the Babylonians first created the zodiac, astrology was further developed during the

Roman Empire. An astronomer, mathematician, and geographer by the name of Ptolemy was born in 100 A.D. While famous for his geocentric theory of the universe, Ptolemy is also one of the most influential figures when it comes to astrology. In the book *Tetrabiblos*, Ptolemy inscribed the practice and beliefs of western astrology. This book is still one of the most authoritative works and is a must-have for anyone who wishes to study the subject.

While the work of the Babylonians and Ptolemy would dominate astrology for the Western world, in Asia, a different zodiac dominates. The Chinese zodiac works almost identically to the Babylonian zodiac, though there are some differences. While both use constellations, the Babylonian version uses both humanoid and animalistic interpretations of said constellations. Additionally, the names of each sign is Latin for another word. For example, Sagittarius is Latin for "archer" and Scorpio is Latin for "scorpion." The Chinese zodiac uses only animals, both for their naming and their symbols. The animals in this zodiac are: Rooster, Dog, Pig, Rat, Ox, Tiger, Rabbit, Dragon, Snake, Horse, Goat, and Monkey. Additionally, unlike the Babylonian zodiac, which changes over the course of the year, the Chinese zodiac only changes at the end of each

Chinese calendar year. The zodiac still has twelve symbols, but it takes twelve years to go through all of them once. Other than those two major differences, the two zodiacs work similarly enough in modern-day, as both can be used to form predictions for daily life.

However, astrology has fallen much since its historical roots. During the Age of Enlightenment, many of the theories surrounding astrology began to be questioned. While astrology did compose of the zodiac and its predictions, the subject also was the source for all astrological knowledge, including planetary alignment and rotational positions. This included Ptolemy's geocentric model, which early astronomers began to pick apart even before the Age of Enlightenment. However, this Age of Reason began to tear down the concepts of mysticism and spirituality to focus more on scientific analysis. While religion was still important to many of the Enlightenment's thinkers, with the consensus saying that all religions should be tolerated, the authority behind astrology began to fade away.

It was only recently that astrology began to regain the attention of the general public. Astrology returned in the 20th century, though in a much smaller format. In the past, the zodiac predictions were typically applied to large populations. Nowadays, the zodiac has been reduced to predicting individual human behavior, with daily horoscopes offering predictions and advice to individuals. These predictions can be very extensive, with some being applied to workplace relations and romantic compatibility. However, those who do practice it are often seen as being ridiculous, claiming that you can't predict things from planetary alignments.

Numerology

While magick consists of a lot of physical items, runes also play an important part when it comes to spellcasting. These symbols carry weight on the spiritual level, and such symbols come in various forms. One set of runes that many might find unorthodox to use for magick is numbers. Numerology uses numbers in order to make predictions in a similar way astrology does with the stars.

The history surrounding numerology is as complex as witchcraft. Multiple civilizations have employed a form of numerology as a way to diviniate their actions. One of the most popular versions, Pythagorean numerology, came from the observations created by a Greek philosopher by the name Pythagoras. He was renowned for his developments in mathematics, astronomy, and music theory. His study of mathematics led him to develop his numerology method, where a person uses both their name and their date of birth to make predictions about their life. This was done through two different equations.

The first equation requires one to convert the month, day, and year into a singular number. This is done by first converting the month into its numerical equivalent (i.e. January would be one, February would be two). Then each digit has to separate from their whole number (i.e. 1953 would separate into one, nine, five, and three). Then all of the numbers are then added up. This process repeats until the resulting number is either a singular digit or it becomes what is considered a Master Number which are numbers that have significance within a numerology system. For Pythagorean numerology, these are the numbers 11 and 22.

The second technique requires the use of one's full name. In order for this process to begin, the person has to replace each letter with a numerical equivalent. While this may seem difficult already, there is a second layer to this. Instead of simply replacing the letter with its numbered position, Pythagorean numerology limits the letter to a single digit number. In order for this to work, the sequence starts with one for "A", ends with nine for "I", then resets the counter to one for "J." This has to be done with a person's full name. Once that is done however, the process is simple. Add up the single digits together repeatedly until you reach a single number for each part of the name. Then add those digits together until you reach a Master Number or a single digit.

These two equations have different purposes according to Pythagoras. The first equation is used to predict one's path in life, offering insight into one's personality, beliefs, and skills. The second equation is used to help determine what will help a person reach their destiny. The single digits and Master Numbers all have different meanings depending on the equation. These equations were adapted as time went on, as Pythagoroas existed around 600 to 500 B.C. and the original was based on the Greek calendar and alphabet.

However, while the Pythagorean form of numerology is one of the most popular versions, it is not the oldest. The Chaldean version of numerology predates Pythagoras, originating from a group of people living in Babylonia. For the most part, Pythagorean and Chaldean numerology systems work the same with two key differences. Chaldean numerology only goes up to eight, not nine. Additionally, unlike Pythagorean numerology, the Chaldean system uses a nonconsecutive numbering system. For example, the letter "F" is turned into an eight, not six. The second difference is that the Chaldean system has a third equation associated with it. This equation is done by translating each letter in a person's full name to their numerical equivalent and adding it up. The resulting number is not reduced, as this double digit has its own meaning attached to it, usually pertaining to events that haven't happened yet in one's life.

Another version of numerology was created by early Hebrews. This system of numerology, Kabbalah numerology, is nearly the exact same as Pythagorean numerology. The only difference is that Kabbalah numerology only cares about a person's name, ignoring the date of birth entirely.

An additional system is Tamil numerology, which was made by a group of people in India who share the same name. This system has the exact same letter to number system as Chaldean numerology, but has two additional equations. While both systems have the name sum equation, Tamil numerology includes a reading for the sum of a person's birth date. These readings come from both the number day itself (i.e. the sixth or the seventh of a month) and the birth date in full.

Numerology, just like witchcraft, has a complex history and multiple systems to consider. While they come from separate sources and have varying readings, most claim to come from a similar source. The source of power does vary a bit, but it is usually associated with vibrations. These vibrations aren't literal vibrations, instead taking more of a mental force, one that exists subtly in everyone's life, even if they don't realize it. Through the vibrations of these numbers, magick is created, and through it we are able to predict or analyze a person's personality, dreams, and challenges they might encounter in the future.

CHAPTER 2
Materials

In modern culture, stories depict spells being sent out through wands or overly large staffs, magical energy sparking and crackling to life in the air around them. Other stories simply have someone wave their hands around in a certain motion to send out energy. Out of the two, the former is much more accurate to one's manipulation of magick, though it is far from the truth when it comes to presentation. Most spells don't use sticks to direct them, and many don't require a person to be in the same room as their target. Instead, what makes those interpretations more accurate is the use of physical objects. While some spells may not require items, the vast majority of them do. Likewise, not every spell shares the same required materials, so knowing what items are required is important.

Due to the nature of magick, mixing random

materials together may not be the best idea. One can easily claim that you need candles, crystals, and herbs, but what can't be easily explained is the meaning behind these items. Each one has a symbolic meaning attached to them, making it important that one pays attention to any spell recipe they come across. Using the wrong materials for a spell could cause unpredictable consequences, especially if you replace one material with a material that symbolizes its direct opposite.

Other items you may need for spellcasting include incense, rope, string, and, yes, sticks. The type of paper may also be important, as many say that parchment paper is the best or only way to cast spells. For beginners, a lot of these items can be found online, as there are online stores that sell spellcasting materials. Just be careful with some of the materials.

Candles

Whenever witches are portrayed as vile hexers, candles are not far behind. Most often, candles are shown around a pentagram with a group of spellcasters summoning a demon from whatever underworld that universe has. Despite this negative connotation, candles are important for spellcasting. More importantly, their use goes beyond summoning spirits or, more oftenly shown, demons. However, like everything else in the spellcasting ritual, the type of candle you use is important. This can include anything from their size to their shape, and even to the candle's scent. However, the most obvious difference in a candle's purpose comes from their color.

White Candles

The color white, in terms of color spectrum, reflects all colors in equal amounts. White candles fit a similar role, where they can be used in replacement of another color. However, such a tactic is not suggested if you want a very potent effect. It can do any candle's job, but other candles do specific tasks better. That is not to say that white candles are entirely worthless when compared to other candles, as white candles do specialize in certain spells.

Protection is one such aspect. Just as the color white repels light, white candles reflect negativity and ill omens. In crafting or focusing on spells that are meant to protect yourself or a loved one, white candles are the way to go. Additionally, white candles can heal or cleanse negativity from a space or person if it would be too late to cast a protection spell. Such cleanses can help improve a person's mood and allow their mind to be free of doubts and pessimistic misconceptions.

Black Candles

Because they are considered opposites in many circumstances, one may expect that black candles are harmful in nature. The truth is the exact opposite. Not to say the colors themselves don't act as opposites. Unlike the color white, which reflects all light, the color black absorbs all light. In practice though, black candles are used to absorb negative energy, focusing all that negativity into itself. This inverse method produces the same overall result to a white candle in terms of negativity removal. However, black candles are considered more effective when it comes to protection, as they absorb the problem, not simply repel it.

Red Candles

Red candles have two sides to them. On one side, red candles can be used to invoke inner strength and passion. Spells meant to boost confidence and courage will often employ red candles. On the other side, red candles are associated with something more promiscuous. Red candles are often used in spells to help boost physical performance, and that performance includes the bedroom. Mind you, spells aren't powerful enough to coerce people to go to bed with you (nor should you ever try even if they did), but they can help make the experience more enjoyable.

Orange Candles

While red candles boost confidence in physical activities, orange candles are used to boost emotional drive. Spells employing orange candles are usually meant to increase one's ambition and good fortune. They can also be used to increase one's energy if they feel drained after a taxing experience, such as a long day after work or after hearing sad news about a celebrity. Many also claim that orange candles can be used to increase one's joy, though that quality could be attributed to their energy rejuvenation property. The lack of energy could feel uncomfortable to some, so a reverse to that condition would in turn improve a person's mood.

Yellow Candles

Just like the other warm colors, yellow candles are meant to boost an aspect of oneself. Specifically, yellow candles are used to increase one's mental capabilities. Spells using these candles can boost focus, intuition, and aid in recalling events, a perfect combination if one is expecting to face a mental test in the future. Other spells using such candles help improve one's creativity, allowing for new ideas to blossom. This creativity is not limited to artistic ventures, as a sales pitch needs as much creativity as a short story. The only difference between them is that a sales pitch is trying to convince people it's true.

Green Candles

Green candles are used in spells aimed at increasing one's bounty. What this "bounty" entails depends on the spell. This can include some traditional prospects, such as fertility or better harvests. Other prospects include financial wealth or increasing one's luck. Green candles can also be used as a way to rejuvenate oneself or help nurture personal growth. If a spell requires something to increase, usually a green candle is involved.

Blue Candles

Blue candles are usually meant for spells that attempt to calm a person. While white candles specialize in countering negative thoughts, blue candles are specialized in countering angry thoughts. Spells using blue candles are often centered around finding inner peace and to center oneself from any thoughts that could result in actions you might later regret. Beyond relieving anger, this inner peace can also grant wisdom, truthful insight, and inspire loyalty between two people. Because of this, spells pertaining to such qualities usually use blue candles.

Purple Candles

Purple candles are most often used for more spiritual spells. These spells can include anything from delving into ancient wisdom, allowing further insight into a certain situation, or in rare cases allowing a person to have visions. These spells are often harder to do as it takes a lot of dedication to pull these off correctly. Alternatively, purple candles are used to increase one's self esteem and decrease stress. Notably, spells meant to counter insomnia regularly use purple candles.

Pink Candles

Pink candles are similar to red candles in the fact that they both deal with love. However, red candles focus on the physical aspects of love. Pink focuses on the emotional side of love, with spells focused on growing a bond between individuals. This bond doesn't have to be romantic, however. Spells using pink candles can range from helping to find new friends to cementing the bond between two partners. These spells aren't mind control, so don't assume that these can make someone madly fall in love with someone else. Spells using pink candles can also be focused on oneself if needed.

Pink candles can promote compassion, self-love, and increase one's empathy.

Brown Candles

Brown is a very earthly color, only rivaled by the color green. Because of this, brown candles are usually used in spells concerning nature or stability. When it comes to its nature half, brown candles are more often used in spells concerning animals, usually to establish a bond with them. In terms of stability, brown candles are often used to bring someone back down to earth. While other candles are specialized in finding inner stability, brown candles are often used in spells concerning the environment around them. In some sense, brown candles could be seen as the opposite of purple candles. While purple candles provide spiritual wisdom, brown candles offer earthly advice. If you plan on doing a spell that requires a purple candle, it might be wise to have a brown candle on hand to recenter yourself.

Silver Candles

Silver candles in some Wiccan circles are considered the most divine. This is because silver is said to represent the Goddess, a deity whose nature varies slightly from coven to coven. However, Wiccans that create altars usually have a silver candle on it in order to share their faith. Beyond that, silver candles are used in spells meant to aid someone's intuition and protect them from unwanted chaos. Sometimes gray can be used in place of silver, but there is some debate about whether or not the two shades mean the same thing.

Crystals

Crystals are a bit of a complex issue when it comes to spellcasting. On the one hand, some claim being in the mere presence of the crystals can cause their effects to go off. On the other hand, some claim that you need to do a ritual for it to work. On a random third hand, you have those, including other spellcasters, claiming that crystals don't work at all. In truth, this debate is a complex one, and the nature of each gemstone varies from type to type. Just be wary when purchasing one if you do, as some crystals could be fake.

Crystals and gemstones are often given healing properties, aiding people fight off stress and illness. However, despite the nature of these stones, it needs to be said that you should still go to a doctor if you are sick. Crystals can aid in healing, but when it comes to illness, nothing is stronger than medicine. Think of gemstones as support that helps you on your road to recovery. Medicine is still the car you need to drive down that road.

Another thing about crystals is the fact that there are a lot of them out there. The sheer number of possible choices as well as some differing opinions about certain gemstones makes it hard to make an entire list detailing each and every one. So instead, here are some popular crystals and what they are used for:

- **Agate:** A multicolored stone that is used to help heal old wounds and to help aid in accepting one's own feelings. It is also used to better one's sleep, both in terms of dreams and the amount of energy the person has the following morning.
- **Amber:** In truth, this isn't a crystal, but a fossilized substance that comes from tree sap. However, the transformative nature of this material means that it is often used to turn negative energy into positive energy.
- **Amethyst:** A purple crystalline quartz, amethyst is used primarily to aid in relaxing one's mind from stress or anxiety. It aims at increasing one's focus while keeping them calm.
- **Garnet:** This red gemstone is often associated with blood, but not in the harmful sense. Instead it is meant to ease

a person of any pain that might come from any blood problems they may be experiencing.
- **Jade:** A gemstone once used for a variety of tasks, it is now used to help a body's natural healing process, specifically when it comes to the internal parts of the body.
- **Rose Quartz:** A pink quartz, this gemstone focuses on helping form bonds with other people. Whether it be romantic love or friendship, this gemstone aids in creating relationships with other people.
- **Sapphire:** A gemstone that is typically blue, sapphires are often associated with wisdom and spiritual knowledge. Having one may aid you in finding the right words to say and wisdom to back those words up.

These are only some examples and not everyone agrees about their usage. You might have to experiment with crystals to see which ones actually have magick properties and which ones are just duds.

Herbs

Like crystals, there are so many herbs that listing them off one by one could and has filled up books. Unlike crystals, however, more practitioners accept the authority of herbs when it comes to their use in rituals. That being said, you shouldn't go out in the wild to collect herbs if you are new to pharmacognosy and botany as you might pick up dangerous plants by mistake. Additionally, while you can grow your own herbs, you aren't really expected to as a beginner. Do not worry though. Plenty of websites sell herbs at decent rates. All you have to do is know which herbs you are looking to use and a way to keep your herbs organized.

Other books are dedicated to the planting, nurturing, harvesting, and preparation of herbs for ritualistic use. However, here are some common herbs you might find in starter kits and their intended usage:

- **Alfalfa:** This herb is used in spells that are meant to protect the caster from poverty and hunger. While it could be considered a herb used for prosperity spells, the herb is mostly specialized in spells combating poverty and hunger specifically.
- **Bay Leaf**: These leaves are used in spells relating to cleansing a space of negative energy. It can also be used to invoke prophetic dreams when placed under a

pillow.
- **Catnip:** This plant's relationship with cats makes it a perfect component for spells concerning cats. However, it can also be used in spells meant to improve mood, beauty, and love.
- **Comfrey:** This herb is used in spells meant to protect oneself during travel. This is most often done by wearing the plant, or putting a bit of it in one's luggage to protect it. It can also be used in spells dealing with money, primarily when land is involved. However, never put comfrey in your mouth. The plant is highly toxic and has the potential to cause liver failure.
- **Dandelions:** This plant actually has different uses depending on which part you use. The roots are often associated with protection from nightmares and are used in spells for spiritual assistance. The leaves are used in spells meant to fight off and heal the effects caused by negativity.
- **Eucalyptus:** The leaves of this plant are used for healing spells and spells used to maintain health. This extends to mental and emotional health, and it can aid in resolving personal conflicts when placed inside an amulet. That being said, you

shouldn't consume the leaves. The herb is toxic and can result in horrible side effects if ingested.
- **Hyssop:** Considered to be one of the most potent purification herbs, this plant is often used to clean a caster's temple, tools, and the caster themselves. It can also be hung around the home to cleanse a space of negativity and ill intent.
- **Lavender:** This flower is used in a whole range of spells, from offering pleasant sleep to healing negative wounds. The herb is also known to bring peace and harmony within one's home and oneself. It can also be used in love spells.
- **Mint:** This plant is often used in spells involving protection, healing, and increasing wealth.
- **Mugwort:** This plant is used primarily in divination, either it be through visions or dreams. This can either be used directly in a spell or used to cleanse or empower other materials used in such spells. When carried, the herb is said to increase lust, fertility, mental wellness and physical wellness.
- **Nettle:** The leaves of this plant are used to remove morbid thoughts and fears

from one's mind and to strengthen the will of the caster. Spells using this herb are meant to aid a person deal with stressful or dangerous situations.
- **Peppermint:** This herb can be used as incense to heal a home of sickness and negative energy. However, the true strength of peppermint lies with its power to boost the strength of other spells. Specifically spells involving love and abundance. This is commonly done by wearing peppermint along with other herbs.
- **Rose:** The petals of this flower are used in spells focused on love and relationships. These relationships don't have to be romantic in nature, but the spells using roses are meant to create a lasting bond between two people.
- **Rosemary:** This herb is often worn to improve a person's memory. It can also be burned to purify a home of negativity and is often used in an infusion to purify one's hands in order to strengthen healing spells. You shouldn't consume the plant at any time as it is toxic to humans.
- **Sage:** The leaves of this plant are used for personal purification and overall

increase in a person's wellbeing. It also repels negative energy associated with grief and loss. A special use of this herb is for a wish granting ritual. By writing a desire on a leaf and placing it under a pillow, the wish will come true if the caster dreams of their wish for three nights in a row.
- **St. John's Wort**: This herb is used in protection and banishing spells aimed at blocking out negative or evil energy. Is also used for simple rituals such as being worn to protect the wearer from cold or fevers. A quick disclaimer is that this herb can be poisonous if consumed in moderate amounts. It can also cause sun sensitivity if it makes contact with skin. Handle this herb with care.
- **Yarrow:** This flower is often associated with love and marriage, and most spells using it pertain to such. Some claim that making a marriage sachet or charm using a yarrow keeps a marriage standing for seven years by protecting the couple from harmful influences. Other spells using yarrow focus on inspiring courage and confidence within the user, allowing them to face their fears.

While this is not a complete list, this should be

enough for you to understand what the materials within a starting kit are meant for. Additionally, this should also show that some of the plants used for rituals are dangerous if consumed and some may be dangerous to rub on oneself. If you don't know if a plant is safe or not, don't put it in your mouth, even if a ritual has it as one of its steps.

Other Items

The basic components of spells are good on their own for certain rituals. However, there are other tools of the trade that might be needed depending on the spell's purpose. Some items all casters need is a ceremonial knife, a small knife meant to cut herbs, and a fireproof bowl. The second and third one is for practical reasons, as you might not want to use the same knives used for cooking food on your herbs, or vice versa, and rituals involving fire can be dangerous if not isolated in a fireproof item. The ceremonial knife may seem nefarious to some. Remember though, this isn't a movie. The knife isn't used for cutting in the majority of spells, but instead is used as a symbol for something else.

While certain components are meant to aid in divination, the heavy lifters of this practice are often something else. Tarot cards, runes, and scrying all are used for divination, so spells conducting such acts usually involve one of them. Tarot cards are the most popular of these forms of divination, and it is easy to see why. Not only are they easy to understand, but there are also many versions of tarot cards that it is easy to make a collection out of the various iterations.

Runes and scrying are less popular ways of looking into the future. Runes are symbols placed on a certain material (usually stone) that are shuffled and tossed. Where and how they land is then used to make predictions about the future. Scrying is a bit more complex to explain as there are many methods one can conduct scrying. However, unlike rune reading and tarot cards, scrying usually involves one or two objects handled in a way to invoke prophetic readings.

Another item that might be needed is a wand of some kind. If you remember earlier, this book previously poked fun at the fact most media portrays wands making magic appear out of thin air. That criticism still stands. Wands do not spew out magic like a firework display. Instead, the wand serves a purpose akin to the ceremonial knife; it is a symbol. However, acquiring a wand can be tricky, as many claim the most potent wands are the ones you make yourself. As this guide is for beginners, it is not recommended you try making a wand for your first spell. Get a handle on your magick before making one, as the wand itself has no magickal properties of its own.

Finally, once you wish to expand your knowledge even further, it will be time for you to get more books on the subject of magick and spells. Or, if you want to experiment a bit, having a journal recording what you find works best for you is a good idea to keep track of your findings. Both may be needed in the future, especially if you want to recall a ritual that worked well for you before. Keeping track this way also enables you to know which components you need to stock up on.

CHAPTER 3
Preparation

Once all materials are gathered, the next step is to prepare the casting of the spell. Preparation can be an entire task in itself depending on the specificity of the spell. Certain spells require a specific location or time of day in order to work. Additionally, the date itself may hold importance for the ritual to be successful. For example, during a full moon, many believe that energy coming from the Moon is at its strongest. To capture this increase in energy, some place jars of clean water in a location exposed to the moon in order to absorb some of the energy it transmits. This exposure leads to the creation of moon water, which can be used for healing spells, a cleansing ritual, or just general use.

If there isn't a location specified for the best results from a spell, you can conduct it in any place that is quiet where you can concentrate.

However, even if a spell doesn't have a specific location, spells typically work better if the location reflects the target of your spell. If your spell is about yourself or another person, being indoors may make more sense. The spell could be further strengthened if the room is significant for the target of the spell, such as a room they have a fondness for. Alternatively, if the spell is associated with nature and animals, casting the spell outdoors may make more sense, with the environment surrounding the caster reflecting the target's natural environment. For example, if the spell is for the wellness of a pet turtle, a lake or pond would be preferable over a forest or an open plain.

Once you know when and where you want to cast the spell, the next step is considering the spell's true intention. While you may have a general idea about what type of spell you want to cast, you will need to have a focused intention when you cast it. Having it written down somewhere or affirming to yourself that this is what you want out of the spell will help keep it focused when you actually cast it. However, while it should be focused, it shouldn't be specific. Spells are generally not powerful enough to alter the world in precise ways. Spells influence the world as it stands instead of bending reality to fit a person's intentions. If you want the spell to give you $3000 over the span of three days by having someone pay you $1000 each day, the spell will not work because that small influence would have to shift too many things. Instead, have the spell's intention be something more general.

CHAPTER 4
Conducting the Ritual

Due to the wide variety of spells, trying to declare an exact way to conduct one is hard to do. Some spells have spoken parts, so making sure you have a clear throat is important. Other times, spells require the caster or casters to move around. In such instances, having enough room to conduct the spell is important. Most spells require high concentration, so making sure you aren't interrupted or distracted is also important. In some ways, casting a spell is the easiest part. If you are following the instructions of another caster, it should be easy as long as everything is set up correctly. If you are attempting to cast a spell of your own creation, it would be better if you wrote the instructions down beforehand in preparation of finally casting it.

A standard step in many spells that could be taken, but is not required, is to make a magick circle. A magick circle is intended to boost one's spell in exchange for additional preparation. In order to create one, you need a purification tool or spell ready, something to form the circle, and the items you need for the other spell you want to cast. Start by purifying the room you wish to cast the spell in. This cleanses the room of negative energy so the circle can amplify positive energy. Then place the items you need for the other spell in the center of where you want your circle to be. This works as an altar, with your intentions being forced onto that central point. After everything is in place, form the circle. This can be done by drawing on the floor or placing items around the perimeter of the desired circle. Limit the material used to something that can be easy to clean, as the circle must be broken at the end ritual in order to work. If you are conducting the spell outside, natural objects like sticks and stones can work to form the circle. Just make sure there is enough room for you to be inside the circle when you are done forming it.

When conducting a ritual, never end the casting prematurely or get distracted. The spell will fail and you will have to start the process all over again. Additionally, there is a chance that the spell may backfire if it is interrupted. If it does, don't worry. You won't find yourself in a movie plot where you are targeted by vengeful spirits or demons. Most likely, it will just cause some minor inconvenience to occur. Still, to stop yourself from repeating a spell's process over and over again, ensure you are comfortable before casting a spell. This is especially true if you are conducting the spell outside, as being too hot or too cold can ruin concentration. On the day you plan on conducting a spell outside, check weather reports before properly dressing for the ritual. Remember, the best way to cast a spell is to focus on your intentions and remove as many distractions as possible.

Once the spell is completed, clean up and simply wait for the results or cast another spell. It may take some time for the spell to come to fruition, so don't expect immediate results. While repeated casting may strengthen it, casting the same spell multiple times on the same day will not result in any noticeable differences. Give it some time before trying the same spell again. If you have a magick circle, make sure to break it during cleanup. Magick circles buildup energy, so not breaking the circle keeps the spell's energy locked within that space.

If you wish to cast more than one spell, make sure they don't conflict with one another while casting inside a magick circle. Conflicting intentions may result in nothing happening or some middle ground that weakens both spells. Even if you think the two spells don't contradict, it may be safer to simply finish the process of one spell, break the circle, then wait a minute or two before doing the second one. Even if you aren't casting in a magick circle, it may be better to keep two spells about vastly different things away from each other. Two conflicting spells may result in something neither intended.

CHAPTER 5
Spells

As mentioned throughout this book, there are many types of spells one can cast. Just like their components, these types vary from each other and some are casted differently than the vast majority of spells. Additionally, some types of spells have more power than others depending on their relationship with the natural world. Magick is usually associated with universal energy, something that is not inherently part of man-made designs. Due to this, spells concerning man-made items or structures may not be as effective when compared to naturalistic spells. This doesn't make those types of spells worthless, but it does mean spells asking for material things or status are relatively weaker compared to spells that aim at performance, emotion, or one's environment.

Purification Spells

The only spell that never needs a magick circle, purification spells are counters to ill intents, negativity, and dark spirits. The actual target of these spells can vary from small items to large rooms to even people. There is no way such spells can backfire as their purpose is to remove negative elements from a person, space, or object. If the spell fails, it most likely just means the caster will have to try again.

The only restriction that is associated with these types of spells is that you will most likely have to be near the target of the spell in order for it to work the best. Unlike other spells, purification spells don't typically work indirectly. When you cleanse something, it is cleansed almost immediately. This immediate result has the trade-off that the range of the spell is severely limited. Think of it like an explosion. Purification spells have an explosive amount of energy, removing all negativity from the vicinity. The further away something is, the less likely the explosion will be effective.

There is one subject that is a point of contention when it comes to purification spells. That point is the question if purification spells or healing spells should be used to help treat disease. There is no clear answer to that question, as some claim that purification spells help while others claim that healing spells are better. While neither are a replacement for medicine, it is still an argument one can have when it comes to spell choice. In addition, due to the complex nature of humans, purification spells may have a harder time removing negative thoughts from a person. For example, if you cast a purification spell at a pessimist with an aim to remove that person's negativity, that pessimist will not be affected as that negativity is part of that person's pessimistic personality.

Healing Spells

Healing spells are targeted at healing the body, mind, spirit, or a combination of the three. It should be clear that these aren't a full replacement for medical or psychological help. No spell is powerful enough to alter the body or mind in that way. What they can do is provide relief, comfort, and aid in the healing process. While they might not be powerful enough to cure an illness, they can be the tipping point that allows someone to recover faster.

The materials used in healing spells change a bit depending on what you want to heal. For example, if you wish to heal someone's spirit, you might want to use a purple candle due to their spiritual significance. For the body, a red candle is more appropriate as they are used in spells associated with physical performance, which includes a body's natural inclination to heal itself. Think about what you intend to heal with this spell and base your materials off that aspect.

Protection Spells

Protection spells are similar to healing spells as they can be applied to the body, mind, and spirit. However, unlike healing spells, protection spells can also be applied to places and objects. Additionally, unlike healing spells, which only deal with the aftermath of an issue, protection spells are meant to prevent bad things from occurring. Even if a bad thing does happen, protection spells still lessen the impact of the event to reduce the amount of harm done.

Like other spells, protection spells can also have a delayed effect. Let's say you plan on traveling and you wish to feel a bit more secure in your travels. Casting a protection spell can help protect you on your travels before you even go on it. That being said, there isn't a noticable difference between a spell aimed at a later date and a spell done at the same time as the action. In other words, if you forget to cast a protection spell before doing something, you can still cast it to get the same amount of protection from it.

As long as the ritual is properly done, a caster should get the same amount of protection from a spell every time.

Love Spells

As mentioned previously, magick can't control minds. Fictional stories regularly paint love spells or potions as this, even if the use of it is supposed to be "funny." True love spells don't work like that. Love spells actually come in two types: discover love spells and strengthen love spells.

Discover love spells are spells focused on finding a companion. While this doesn't have to be a romantic partner, it most often is, though there are spells out there aimed at finding new friends. Discover love spells are like bird calls: they are signals aimed at helping the speaker (or caster in this case) find a partner. If you are on dating apps or similar services, the change will probably be unnoticable. These spells focus on helping you discover possible connections with the people around you. If you are seeking a romantic partner while using dating services, you are already seeking to find these connections. Sending out more signals isn't going to help that much.

Even if you have no use for discovering love

spells, most people can find use in strengthening love spells. Strengthening love spells are spells focused on bolstering the bonds between two people. The bond doesn't have to be romantic, but it is recommended that both parties within the relationship are present for the spell. If both are present and accepting of the spell's power, the spell itself will become more powerful compared to ones done by only one person in the relationship. Even if only one person of the relationship is casting, both sides have to be receptive to the spell's intentions. If the person targeted by the spell doesn't want to have a strengthened bond with the caster, or vice versa, the spell will not work.

Prosperity Spells

Prosperity spells are an umbrella term for spells that are meant to increase an aspect of life. This is intentionally vague as what that thing is depends on the spell. For example, some spells focus on increasing fertility or aiding the growth of plants while other spells focus on financial gain. These spells focus on physical parts of life either by directly providing the requested goods or by influencing factors to increase the probability of gaining what one desires. These spells are technically the weakest type of spells.

Unlike other spells that influence things on their

own or help benefit preexisting systems, prosperity spells require the caster to do something to aid it after casting it. For example, if the caster casted a spell to increase their harvest and do nothing to tend to their plants, the spell will not work as the plants the spell was aimed at weren't properly cared for. In order to get the most out of the spell, the caster would still need to take care of the plants. Prosperity spells work on future actions, not actions of the present or the past. This makes them the weakest as their effect may hardly be noticeable depending on the target of the spell.

Invigoration Spells

Invigoration spells is an umbrella term for spells that are meant to boost an aspect of oneself. This could be anything from energy to mood to creativity to even physical performance. These spells help the caster gain focus and clarity while also allowing them to push their body to the limits. Like with healing spells, these types of spells change depending on the materials used to cast them. If you want to boost more than one aspect of yourself, you will need materials reflecting both aspects you wish to increase.

A thing to note is that invigoration spells don't add anything. They simply reveal what doubt hides and releases the true strength that lies within the caster. So no, these spells do not replace workouts, study habits, or good diets. They only allow the caster to work with all they have, something that life can cloud through everyday problems. While some may argue that invigoration spells are weaker than prosperity spells, the truth is that doubts and a lack of confidence can be very detrimental to performance. Having something to boost confidence can provide an immediate and noticeable improvement compared to spells that may have effects that aren't noticeable.

Divination Spells

Divination spells are focused on gaining new insights about yourself or the world around you. While this can be about the future, divination spells do not need to focus on it. They could help figure out one's current relationship with a coworker or they can help provide a new perspective on a recent event. Divination is simply aimed at exploring the unknown, with the spells associated with it aimed at answering the mysteries the unknown holds.

As mentioned previously, divination spells have their own unique materials such as tarot cards and rune stones. However, they are not the only materials used for divination spells, so solely relying on them can be very limiting. Take tarot cards for example. While they can brush upon a person's past, present, and future, they can't focus on any one thing. They can give general observations and allow one to reassess their knowledge on certain events, but they don't target events directly. While there are other spells that can do that, tarot readings aren't as focused as one might wish them to be.

Tarot Cards

Tarot card readings are often the poster child of divination. There are many ways to use tarot cards for divination with the most commonly portrayed method being a three card spread where the past, present, and future are laid out in front of you. However, despite this popular picture, tarot cards are a bit more complicated than that. This is not simply because there are techniques that use more than three cards, but because those readings solely use the major arcana cards.

A full tarot card set includes seventy-eight cards, twenty-two belonging to the major arcana while fifty-six belong to the minor arcana. Major arcana are the most popular and most impactful cards. These cards are meant for large scale questions about one's personal life and one's potential future. Unlike the minor arcana, the major arcana all have their own individual names, such as "The Hermit," "The Hanged Man," and "The World." While some have similarities, all of the major arcana cards are seen as their own entities and are only grouped together due to their importance.

The minor arcana is something you don't see a lot in the media. Like a set of playing cards, the minor arcana is divided into four groups. While their names can be different depending on the set you are using, the original and standard names for them are wands, cups, swords, and pentacles. These sets, following the same number and name system as a regular deck, are meant to answer more day-to-day questions and minor concerns. Each set deals with a different aspect of one's life, with each card relating to their set's meaning. Wands focus on creativity and ambition, cups are focused on emotions and relationships, swords focus on intuition and finding truth, and pentacles focus on material things and ways to get them. Major and minor arcana can be used together in certain readings, but there are plenty that just focus on one and not the other.

Rune Reading

Rune divination spells are not as popular as tarot cards, but can still be used to answer questions or make predictions of the future. The most popular form of rune reading is based on the Norse runic alphabet, which consists of 24 symbols, each with their own meaning. While some symbols may seem odd to certain people, others are very similar or exact copies of letters found in the Latin alphabet. For example, there is an "X" and an "R" in the Norse runic alphabet. Each of these has a secondary name attached to them, with "X" having the name "Gebo" and "R" having the name "Raidho."

Divination using rune stones comes in a variety of ways, though the simplest is by using only one rune. The way to conduct this form of divination is by first getting a bag full of the runes and shaking it in one hand. Carefully consider the question you wish to answer before putting your hand in the bag. Without looking, pick out a stone that feels right to pull out. Once you pull it out, notice everything about the rune. Was the rune facing you when you pulled it out? Was the rune upside down? Once you take note of how it was pulled out, reference the rune's meaning in order to make an interpretation about what the rune meant in relation to your question.

That is one method of using runes for divination. Some rituals use multiple runes, either by tossing the stones out of the bag onto a soft surface or by pulling out multiple stones.

However, like tarot cards, the answers aren't always clear. Runes have multiple meanings. On top of that, while they can be described with common themes, their direct translation can be vague.

For example, Raidho can be interpreted as road or journey. While this may seem obvious in many contexts, you might be confused if you pulled the rune out after asking whether or not someone is into you. Assuming you pulled the rune out while it was facing you and it was right-side up, it could mean that the relationship will be a journey with no clear way of telling whether or not it will end the way you want it. Alternatively, it could mean that the roads the two of you walk on may be parallel, meaning the two of you may not get into a romantic relationship, but a platonic one. Both interpretations are valid, even though they contradict.

Scrying

Scrying is difficult to explain because there are multiple methods one can do in order to scry. Some look into flames for messages while others use a crystal ball or other reflective surface to look for visions. Of the several types, looking into reflective surfaces is considered the most popular and easiest to do. However, no matter what method one takes in order to scry, there are similarities in all scrying spells.

Firstly, like with other spells, scrying requires that the practitioner isn't interrupted. Unlike tarot and rune reading however, scrying can be a very lengthy process. While the other two already discussed forms of divination could reach up to half an hour per session, it is very rare for that to happen. For scrying, thirty minutes may be a little longer than usual, but it shouldn't be unexpected. The reason why is because scrying requires the caster to be in a meditative state. In order for one to properly scry, one has to be in a calm, relaxed state of being. Even once someone is in that state of being, it may take time before the material used actually shows an image or message.

Of course, simply being in a meditative state doesn't help answer a question. To attain visions that answer their question, the caster needs to think about the topic they want answers to while gazing into the object. The way one actually looks at the object shifts from item to item, with some items requiring clear vision while others require the caster to watch with an unfocused stare. Some scrying even requires the caster to observe the exact details of an object to make predictions, though these processes are a bit more advanced. Record your observations and try to interpret what the signs mean once the scrying is complete for the best results.

CHAPTER 6
Spellcrafting

All this information means little if we can't cast a spell ourselves. There are dozens of books filled to the brim with spells, some larger than others. However, since an important part of the craft is making your own spells, this book shall go through the method one can take to make a spell. There will also be an example, as no book about spells isn't complete without having one itself.

Step 1: Determining What You Want

As with all spells, the reason why you want to cast it is because you want something. It doesn't have to be selfish. However, each spell has a desire behind it, and the first step is finding out which one you want to impose. Perhaps you have a sick family member and wish to make them better. A healing spell would work best for you in that case. Maybe you have a rough presentation to show tomorrow, and you want to spend the night practicing to make sure you get it right. An invigoration spell can aid you in focusing on your practice.

While this may seem like a simple step, it is very important you know for sure what you want. Magick and spells reflect the intentions of the caster. If the caster doesn't want the effects of the spell to take hold, either consciously or subconsciously, the spell will most likely fail as the caster wasn't dedicated to the spell's intentions. They don't need to be devoted to the spell, but they should think carefully about whether or not they want what they think they want.

For the purposes of this book, let us make a simple protection spell aimed at keeping us safe at night from burglars.

Step 2: Gathering the Appropriate Material

As mentioned before, most spells have material in one form or another. Making sure you have the right material is important for any caster. This step is basically just the application of Chapter 2, so just use that for reference. That being said, just because a piece of material is meant to aid in a certain type of spell doesn't mean you need that material. In fact, if you believe the spell you wish to cast doesn't need materials, you can skip this step entirely.

For our example, materials will be used just to show how they can be incorporated into a spell. The protection spell shall use a brown or white candle as the main component. Brown due to the earthly nature of this protection and white because that color of candle can take the place of any other candle.

Step 3: Planning Out the Ritual

This is when we decide a time and place to conduct the ritual. Additionally, this is when we write up an incantation to use to help focus our intention towards the spell. This incantation could either be verbal or mentally spoken, but it should be written down for reference. While the time or place could be flexible, the invocation itself should be pretty strict. The strictness helps keep focus, which is important for any spell.

For our protection spell, the invocation shall be, "Of this room, none shall be taken. Of this space, no intruder shall enter. Of my home, let no crime happen."

Step 4: Testing a Spell

Finally, once that is all done, it is time to test the

spell. How you test it really depends on what you want out of the spell. Are you searching for love? Then you most likely would just stay in one room. Are you trying to purify the house? Then perhaps moving through several rooms is appropriate. Is the spell targeted at someone? Then you might want to have a picture or object associated with that person. There isn't really a guide on how to test a spell as it really depends on what *you* think is needed for it.

For the protection spell, since it is to protect the home from burglars, the spell itself will be tested by moving from room to room reciting the incantation.

Step 5: Sharing the Spell

While this step isn't required, you might want to write down and share your spell with other people. Do know if you do this people are going to have mixed reactions. Some will be skeptical, others will be outright dismissive, but there will be those truly interested in the spell you've crafted. As long as you stay respectful and safe, there shouldn't be any problems with sharing your spell.

If you want an example of how to format your spell, here is one way to do it:

Protection From Burglars Spell

During sunset, ignite a brown candle in the furthest room of your house. Recite the following:

"Of this room, none shall be taken. Of this space, no intruder shall enter. Of my home, let no crime happen."

Walk through each room you wish to protect while reciting the phrase, making sure to repeat each time you enter a room you haven't walked through before. Once you reach your front door, blow out the candle and set it down on the floor.

This is only an example and really you can format the written form of the spell in any way you think is most appropriate.

CHAPTER 7
Alternative Magick

As stated earlier, most of the magick described in this book involves the practice of Wicca. However, there are several more types of magickal practices out there. From old practices such as Druidism and Heka to modern structures such as Satanism and Thelema Magick, there are those who conduct magick rituals while not directly associating themselves with Wiccans. Some of these practices have been abandoned, while others have many practitioners in the modern-day. These practices are varied in both history and techniques, as well as what their magick is intended for.

Druidism

Druidism is unique when it comes to fictional depictions. Unlike generic magic, several fictional settings distinguish Druidism as its own thing entirely, treating the group of practitioners differently from other spellcasters. Additionally, while wizards and witches are depicted in numerous ways, Druids are usually restricted to magic related to nature. This includes such things as shapeshifting into an animal and asking nature spirits to aid them in battle. While the literal interpretations and dramatization of such powers are to be expected, the core ideas in fictional Druidism are surprisingly accurate to modern Druidic practices.

"Modern" is the key word that needs to be focused on when talking about Druidism. The Celtic origins of this form of magick lacks written records, meaning all information pertaining to them are either from secondhand accounts or from testimonies of those who keep up the oral tradition of teaching the practice to younger generations. Additionally, like other types of ancient magick discussed later on, there was no unified version of Druidism. While there will still be plenty of discussion about Druidic beliefs, like Wiccans, Druidism is a complex and branching topic that has different interpretations. Additionally, while Wiccans and Druids can be similar in many aspects, the two aren't inherently the same.

While the particulars of Druidism may shift

from group to group, there are some overarching themes present in all of them. Druidism regularly focuses on nature and the wisdom it provides, though how this wisdom is granted varies slightly between interpretations. Sometimes, the wisdom comes from nature spirits. Other times, it is from gods and goddesses. How this wisdom is given is usually consistent, though, with the seeker communing with the giver in a natural setting.

Druidism treats nature differently though from most modern perceptions. Instead of acting as if nature is one unified unit, Druidism is based on regional power. For instance, the wisdom and power present in one forest may not be the same for another forest several miles away, as the needs and ecological balance of these forests could be different in nature. Due to this regional focus, one could argue that even in heavily populated cities one could find nature's wisdom, though it would be harder to do as nature isn't as prominent there.

Another thing that many Druids conduct is the celebration of the solstices and equinoxes as well as four seasonal holidays. One of the more famous of the seasonal holidays is Samhain, as it is on the same day as Halloween. This is no coincidence, as Samhain merged with another holiday, All Hallows' Eve, to become Halloween, with Samhain's influences being seen through the traditions of costume-wearing and trick-or-treating (History.com Editors, 2018a). Other holidays include Imbolc at the start of spring, Beltane at the start of summer, and Lammas near the beginning of autumn. The specific dates for these holidays aren't as clear as Samhain's, which adds further confusion when taking the hemispheres into account.

Other than that, Druidism doesn't really have unifying details, even in its earliest days. Welsh, Scottish, and Irish practitioners all had minor differences between them. While the most obvious would be their location, different terminology was also used between the three groups. For example, some Scottish Druids called spirits or fairies "devils," though they weren't associated with the Christian concept of a devil (Forest, 2020). This expectantly didn't go down well with Christain missionaries, leading to certain Druid groups being accused of malicious witchcraft (Forest, 2020). Additionally, experts of local Druidic practices were called different names. In certain parts of Ireland, Druidic medical experts were called *bean feasa* or "wise-women," while in Britain, they were called "the cunning folk" (Forest, 2020).

On top of different terminology, they also faced different levels of discrimination when engaged with Christians. As stated previously, Scottish Druids calling helpful fairies "devils" caused several of these groups to be persecuted. However, in Wales and Ireland, this problem did not arise as often, with their magick actually being seen as an important part of many local communities (Forest, 2020). Thanks to such groups surviving, modern-day Druidic groups have an easier way to trace back their practices and historians have a better chance to understand Druidic beliefs, though there is still a large lack of historical Druidic records.

The idea of a Druidic group existing in the modern-day may seem like a surprise to some, but the fact is that multiple organizations practicing Druidism exist. One group, the Order of Bards, Ovates, and Druids (OBOD) are based in England and are considered by some to be the largest of these modern groups. The OBOD's website offers more in-depth teachings of Druidry and even offers members the ability to become a "celebrant," a priest of sorts who is "able to design and lead Weddings/Handfastings, Funerals, Baby Namings & other Rites of Passage" (*Our Courses and Membership*, n.d.). Another modern group of Druids is Ár nDraíocht Féin

(ADF), an organization based in the United States. In Irish, the name means "our own magic," though they claim they "incorporate practices from ancient and modern Indo-European cultures including the traditions of Celtic and Norse cultures, Slavic, Baltic, Greek, Roman, Persian, Vedic, and other cultures" (*Ár nDraíocht Féin – Our Own Druidry*, 2022).

However, even in the modern-day, organizations have difficulty agreeing on what defines Druidism. The OBOD considers Druidism to be a loose term that could mean religion, spiritual path, or simply a philosophy. However, the ADF explicitly calls themselves a church, making their view on Druidism different from the OBOD's.

With all that in mind, one might find it hard to actually figure out what would constitute a Druid spell. Fortunately, there are plenty of examples that one can work with. One practice was the memorization and use of hymns, chants, and incantations in a particular verse structure. Ancient Irish Druids used this practice, calling such songs and poems *cetal* or *laedha* structured (Maccrossan, 2002). Poetic language itself, either sung or simply stated, carries the magick in this situation, with the words chosen to create a specific effect. Another thing Irish poets used were "ogams; numerals, ciphers and codes made from notches carved along the straight edge of a twig" meant for divination purposes (Maccrossan, 2002).

Something that fantasy Druids and actual Druids do share is the ability to alter themselves to become an animal. For fantasy Druids, this is literally interpreted as the ability to shapeshift. For real Druids, the rituals and incantations used to invoke this ability alters the mindset of the caster and doesn't actually cause a physical transformation as radical as their fictional counterparts. Real Druids also tend to have more complex rituals. An example of this comes from a healing spell, where a caster dips a rag or clootie in a clean, blessed body of water before washing a sick person with the blessed rag, asking water spirits to bless and cure the ill person (Forest, 2020). The cloth is then hung from a tree, preferably a hawthorn, and left to rot, with the sickness being taken away as the rag decays (Forest, 2020).

While there are many rituals asking nature for aid, the relationship between Druids and nature isn't one-sided. Asking help from nature while neglecting or destroying it often results in a lot of failed spells. A Druid must have a strong, or at least decent, connection with nature, honoring it and asking for aid only when needed. However, beyond not littering and planting trees, there are other ways to become more connected with the land. Altars are a popular choice, as is meditation. Unlike some fictional depictions, the use of technology isn't directly harmful to one's relationship with nature. However, overusing or mishandling technology can weaken one's relationship, such as driving somewhere all the time when you can easily walk to the location. Balance is the key here.

Some may claim that Druid spells and Wicca spells are interchangeable to some extent. To be fair, they are right. Many of the tools, herbs, and methods used to cast Wiccan spells would still find some use in a pure Druidic practice. However, what makes Druids unique is the fact that a Druid never needs to cast a spell to be considered a Druid. Spells aren't required for those who follow the tenets of Druidism, hence why the OBOD recognizes that some people who call themselves Druids simply see it as a philosophy. Not every Druid practices with magick in mind, so even if you aren't interested in or believe in Druidic spells, you could be interested in the more complex nature of Druidic belief.

Heka

Heka is the Egyptian form of magick that draws origins from the god Heka. Due to the nature of Heka, the magick associated with it is directly connected to the old Egyptian deities. Despite this being a very old form of magick, many of the rituals conducted through Heka have similar modern-day examples. Some have argued that Heka has inspired modern-day magic and magick in various ways. Being one of the oldest practices out there, it would make sense if this is true.

One aspect of Heka that is seen in most modern interpretations of magick is the belief that everyone has access to it. While priests and doctors were the primary authorities for the practice, Ancient Egyptian lifestyle catered to the concept that everyone could invoke the power Heka provides. The most common application of this was to wear amulets, which are akin to modern-day charms. These charms were usually meant for protection, though they could be used to invoke other qualities. Additionally, Egyptian Heka might have inspired the eventual popularization of connecting wands to magic, as ivory wands were used during stressful times.

Something that bleeds into popular media

depictions of spellcraft from Heka is the importance of pronunciation. According to Dr. Geraldine Pinch, in order for a spell to work, "all the words, especially the secret names of deities, had to be pronounced correctly" (Pinch, 2011). While this idea does apply to other practices of magick, this concept is more prevalent in media, where magic is more likely to go wild if the speaker mispronounces a word. However, unlike popular media, Dr. Pinch goes further and details that, "Many spells included speeches, which the doctor or the patient recited in order to identify themselves with characters in Egyptian myth" (Pinch, 2011). The purpose of these speech spells were meant to help manifest an outcome similar to the nature of the myth recited. As stated in the quote, this type of ritual was primarily incorporated into healing spells conducted by doctors.

Speaking of healing magick, one might improperly assume that, due to the nature of Heka, the Egyptians would use only spells to deal with illnesses while ignoring medicine. Nothing could be further from the truth. Ancient Egyptian doctors used a combination of healing spells and medical practices to help the ill and wounded. While they did believe evil spirits would cause the illness that must be repelled, they also recognized that such spells didn't stop the physical harm caused by such spirits.

What is unique for Heka compared to many forms of magick practice is that written magick is seen as a highly coveted item. Due to the low rate of literacy in Ancient Egypt, written spells were a rarity as only a select few could write them. This rarity doesn't necessarily make it more powerful. Instead, they were valued for their long-lasting effects. As stated previously, words have magick power in Heka, and this power wouldn't be diluted if it was written on paper. This meant that a written spell would last longer while still holding the strength of a standard ritual. These written spells were often seen as a more powerful alternative to amulets, with written spells being "handed down within families" in order to keep such strong magick on hand (Pinch, 2011).

Heka was a very important thing for Egyptians, even in death. Famously, the Egyptian *Book of the Dead* is filled with spells that were meant to protect a person as they traveled through the afterlife. However, while the popular fascination with mummies have helped bring such a text some popularity, the hyperfixation has limited people's knowledge on the day-to-day practices conducted by regular citizens. While the dead did practice Heka, they were just doing something that they had practiced while they were alive.

Kotodama

Kotodama is a unique form of magick for two reasons. The first is that it is an entirely vocal and written form of magick, with the words themselves being the only thing that truly matters for this type of magick. The second is that it is directly tied to a language, specifically Japanese. Like other forms of magick, the origins of Kotodama are old. Unlike other forms though, Kotodama still has incredible influence over modern culture today in Japan. However, like many cultural things, Kotodama has changed over the centuries due to its connection with the Japanese language.

Before exploring that, we must first discuss what Kotodama is in terms of power. Like most forms of magick, everyone can do it as long as they can speak Japanese. Unlike most forms, additional training isn't required. Instead, the power results in the words you choose to use. According to Kotodama, saying or writing positive words result in positive results. Similarly, the use of negative words results in negative results. While some may associate Kotodama with karma, Kotodama differs in the fact that the target of the words receives the outcome of a person's word choice. If you speak positively about something, they receive a positive result instead of you, and vice versa. While this may all seem simple, the history surrounding what counts as Japanese makes this much harder to pin down.

The birth of Kotodama was caused by a fusion of Shinto, a religion that started in Japan, and *yamato kotoba*, the original language of Japan. In Shinto, it is believed that everything has a spirit attached to it, and this extends to words. In fact, Kotodama translates to the "spirit of language" or "power of language." Kotodama arose alongside Shintoism, with Shinto priests writing spells that sought for divine aid. However, like most languages, what was considered to be "Japanese" changed over time.

The earliest of these changes arrived during the introduction of Chinese words and elements. This form of Japanese, either called Sino-Japanese or *kango*, was created due to the major influence China had over its surrounding nations. While not a direct copy, *kango* added words that were either entirely Chinese or used elements from Chinese vocabulary. However, this adoption was seen as impure by the Shinto priests, who determined that only *yamato kotoba* was able to draw in the power of Kotodama. Despite this, *kango* was still adopted by many Japanese, which helps explain a major change that would happen to Kotodama.

During World War II, the Japanese government wished to strengthen nationalistic zeal in their country. One of the programs the government put in place was to reestablish Kotodama as a major force in Japanese life, claiming that traditional Japanese is, "at the core of the national unity and social virtue that is unique to Japan" (Hosokawa, 2014). However, despite claiming traditional Japanese was the key to unity, the Japanese at this time didn't stick with *yamato kotoba*. Instead, both *kango* and *yamato kotoba* were acceptable forms of Japanese in the eyes of the governing body, expanding the definition of what could be used in Kotodama.

This adoption wasn't entirely isolated though. Just like with Sino-Japanese words before, the Japanese government denounced the use of new words adopted from foreign territories. In this instance, the denounced words were *gairaigo*, words that came from or were heavily influenced by Western countries. Like *kango* words before them, *gairaigo* were seen as impure and therefore didn't have the power of

Kotodama associated with them. Additionally, *gairaigo* words were replaced by Sino-Japanese words.

Kotodama is still culturally important to many Japanese people. Many still connect Kotodama with unity, often using the concept to promote the exclusion of adopted or adoptable foreign words. On a smaller scale, people who believe in Kotodama usually have an aversion to negative words in certain social situations. A common example of this can be seen during weddings, where words that are associated with things ending or separating are avoided at all costs. Kotodama dictates that saying such words can lead to an ill marriage that results in divorce, so attendants at weddings avoid such words as much as possible. In fact, the belief is so strong that the end of a wedding is often called the "opening" (Geeraert, 2020).

Weddings are not the only instances where Kotodama can have a negative influence. During exams, words involving falling or an action that results in one falling are considered dangerous to say or write down as well. This is because literal translations of Japanese equate failing to falling in relation to tests, meaning that saying words associated with falling can result in influences that result in the tester failing

(Geeraert, 2020).

Another thing affected by Kotodama is the reception of numbers. Due to pronunciation, certain numbers are often seen as unlucky due to a word or phrase that is close to the number's pronunciation. Some examples of negative words being associated with numbers include "stillbirth" with the number 43, "death" with the number 4, and "suffering" with the number 9. Due to the numbers being closely related to negative words, those who practice Kotodama usually avoid those numbers, especially in a hospital setting, so be careful when visiting Japan to not say negative or potentially harmful things. Words can be dangerous.

Mageia and Goeteia

Mageia or Goeteia, depending on the era in question, was the Greek term for magick. While both could apply to the Greek tradition of magick, the term "mageia" was actually derived from the Persian term *magos* (*Goêteia Explorations in Chthonic Sorcery*, n.d.). Of the two, Mageia is considered more popular in a historical context as social developments altered the Greek perspective on the subject of magick, partially when it was associated with goeteia (*Goêteia Explorations in Chthonic Sorcery*, n.d.). However, there seems to be no difference in the practice of either version, making it seem more like a branding decision than anything else.

Mageia practices were similar to many other practices in terms of what they were trying to accomplish. There are protection spells, luck spells, curative spells, and spells to increase one's fertility. The Greeks combined both inorganic materials, such as engraved amulets used for protection, and organic materials, such as flowers and plants to cure diseases. One of the most famous recorders of such information was Theophrastus, who was not only a philosopher, but also a botanist who made several observations and possible uses of plants. Some of these usages include getting rid of illness through the use of squill and to use early purple orchid as an aphrodisiac (Hayward, 2020).

A large part of Greek Mageia was a type of practice many might find evil in modern contexts. Amongst the spells and protective amulets, the Greeks also practice cursing to a certain extent. Greek curses usually came in the form of a tablet called a "katara." The curse was intended to weaken a rival or opponent. Additionally, there were figures called "kolossoi" that could be used in a similar manner.

There is a big difference between the two, however. Katara were entirely hostile, meaning that someone making or purchasing one was trying to settle a score. Namely, the power of the katara was to ask for aid from the underworld. By placing the katara in a grave or another hole that goes into the earth, the katara would request that agents from the underworld help harm a person in the living world. Kolossoi, while still being harmful to humans, were also used to bind evil spirits, weakening them in the process. This is because kolossoi are similar to the popular notion of a voodoo doll, though it would be wrong to say that kolossoi work in the exact same way. The most obvious difference between kolossoi and the popular imagination of a voodoo spell is that kolossoi can also target spiritual beings.

Despite not being as famous as other magick, Greeks still use some of the old symbols to this day. A prominent example of this is the evil eye, or *mati*, which is usually symbolized with a blue eye surrounded by a darker blue circle. An evil eye is a simple curse given to someone by way of a vengeful or hostile look that then translates to minor inconveniences for the recipient of the look. A way to counter the curse is to wear a symbol of mati on your person, mostly in the form of an amulet. There are other forms of protection against the evil eye, but an amulet is the most convenient as it doesn't require any additional action after putting it on. However, the evil eye is usually only a danger to those that are really vulnerable.

Mesopotamia Āšipūtu

This type of magick originates from Mesopotamia and, similar to Heka, is directly connected to Mesopotamian religious beliefs. Despite many magick practices being lost to time, Āšipūtu was able to survive thanks to the aid of cuneiform tablets. From those tablets, historians were able to discover an ancient form of magick, though the nature of it is a bit loose. Similar to Japanese Kotodama, Mesopotamian Āšipūtu changed as the civilization changed, though there are some things that are clear about the topic.

For starters, Āšipūtu was divided into four major types: "liminal magic" that was focused on changing a person or an object into something else, "defensive magic" that aimed to remove "an evil" from a targeted person, "aggressive magic" that was meant to increase one's "superiority, strength, and attractiveness," and "witchcraft," which in this case means a form of illegal magick that was meant to cause harm (Schwemer, 2014b). As one can already guess, witches in Mesopotamia have the same negative connotation as they had in several other civilizations in the past. However, unlike their later Christian counterparts, the treatment of witches was quite different.

While both Christians and Mesopotamians were more inclined to believe that women were more often witches, for the Mesopotamians, finding who that was wasn't important. Defensive magic didn't need the name of the witch to deflect harmful magic. In fact, evidence points that spells against witchcraft "emphasize that the identity of the evildoers is unknown to their innocent victim" (Schwemer, 2014a). Mesopotamian defensive spells designed to fight witchcraft regularly reflect the ill intent back on the hostile caster, potentially indicating that such spells work best if the victim of a hostile spell doesn't hold any hostility towards a named individual in case they weren't the ones to cast the spell, but aggression was still held towards their assailant, even if their identity is supposed to be unknown. A common element for anti-witch spells is the destruction of a pair of figurines, one for a male, one for a female (Schwemer, 2014a). This destruction could include torturing the figurines as well, though the destruction was the final catalyst for the spell to take effect.

From this, one could assume that being a witch in this time period was completely safe. While it can be comparably safer compared to other regions, supposed witches could still be sentenced to death. However, the accuser was as in much danger as the accused. If the accuser had no proof that a person was a witch, the supposed witch would undergo a trial to prove their innocence (Schwemer, 2014a). If the accused passed their test, the accuser would be charged with the crime of falsely charging someone of ill deeds and punished accordingly. Unfortunately for the accuser, this most often resulted in death (Schwemer, 2014a). This controlled the number of witch trials, as the accuser was on trial just as much as the one they had accused.

However, so far, only the practitioners of illegal magick have been named. For legal practitioners, there were various names that correlated with their position in society. The āšipu, or ashipu, were the main practitioners of magick, holding a position akin to priests and exorcists. There was a group called the asu, or "physicians," that were similar to the ashipu that focused primarily on fixing illness and other maledictions (Said, 2018). There was also a separate group of divination practitioners called baru, who typically were in elite positions working directly under a king (Said, 2018). All of these practitioners were glorified in Mesopotamian society, though the baru stood out, as the ashipu and asu could take on each others' roles as needed.

Just like how modern historians are able to study Āšipūtu, it is theorized that the practitioners of old were taught through the use of cuneiform texts. This form of teaching allowed for standardization of spellcasting. Assyrians, who lived in Northern Mesopotamia, are a clear example of this standardization, as governing kings commanded the creation of a series of books referred to as "handbooks" to create a canonical and approved form of Āšipūtu (Said, 2018). However, even with this supposed standardization, there is some debate on how strictly these handbooks were practiced. Archeologists have discovered sites where the materials present seem to correspond with a ritual that doesn't perfectly match the phrasing of a cuneiform text about the same ritual (Mirelman, 2018). Sometimes, this variation is so extreme that entire objects used for ritualistic purposes were completely ignored. In one documented instance, ritualistic figurines were placed in "brick capsules," though the purpose of these capsules weren't detailed within a corresponding text (Mirelman, 2018). This gap in knowledge makes it hard for someone to create a modern version of the practice based primarily on historical evidence as there seems to be some variations between what was taught and what was practiced.

Even with these gaps, there are still commonalities that can be gained from the cuneiform texts and physical evidence. As mentioned previously, defensive spells against witches regularly had figurines meant to depict the aggressor, but the use of figurines or similar objects were not limited to that single purpose, however. In fact, according to some researchers, Āšipūtu practitioners believed that images could have a will of their own, exerting such will by influencing the world around them (Said, 2018). An example of this comes in the form of the Iamassu, "massive, winged composite creatures with the head of a man and features of a bull or lion," that were built to guard important entryways from any form of metaphysical threat (Said, 2018). Unlike the figurines used in defensive spells, these statues were much larger, meaning that objects with magick came in a great variety of sizes for the Mesopotamians. However, there does seem to be a correlation with size and power when it comes to such objects.

While large statues made of stone were made to protect places of authority, people of lower social status could gain some protection through the use of guardian clay figures (Said, 2018). These protective idols came in a variety of shapes, though they were mostly "gods, animals, and hybrid creatures" (Said, 2018). Due to the difference in size and materials, it could be guessed that the larger and stronger a protective figure was, the greater the defense it could give against metaphysical threats. This difference in power did little in terms of placement, as even clay figures were put next to doorways and other places considered vulnerable to villainous spirits (Said, 2018). Upon reflection, one could see that the witch figurines that were meant to be destroyed during a defense ritual are an exception to an otherwise benevolent form of defense. This differentiation might be due to how Mesopotamians view illness in the first place.

Like the Egyptians, the Mesopotamians combined magick with medical practices to heal the sick and wounded. In fact, alongside their many cuneiform texts about casting away dark spirits, the Mesopotamians had a vast collection of medical texts, primarily in the form of pharmaceuticals (*Healing and Medicine: Healing and Medicine in the Ancient near East*,

2022). However, the Mesopotamians believed that the root cause of all misfortune and illnesses came from a personal lack of favor from the gods (*Healing and Medicine: Healing and Medicine in the Ancient near East*, 2022). The exact cause for this disfavor could be entirely unintentional, but because it still offended the gods, they would still seek retribution for that act. While demons and spirits could still inflict pain onto a person, it was only when they lost a god's favor was they became vulnerable to such attacks. If they had a god's favor, any metaphysical attack will fail thanks to divine protection. If we relate this back to the destruction of the witch figurines, it could be said that the destruction of such figures was to instill divine justice against those who had tried to take advantage of a person who needed to seek redemption.

Another common practice was the use of amulets and other accessories to protect one's body from malicious forces while outside of one's home. However, unlike the figurines and statues that resembled good deities and creatures, amulets and pendants depicted dark deities and demons (Said, 2018). This was meant to deflect the evil entities, possibly working like a reflection to send such influence elsewhere. Other times, offerings to benevolent deities were marked around the symbol of the dark creature, neutralizing the dark force entirely (Said, 2018). Taking into account that people become vulnerable when they lose favor with the gods, perhaps the use of accessories in this way was meant to provide protection while still keeping face with protective deities. It could be interpreted that placing a divine being on an amulet means you want to drag them around everywhere, which could be seen as rude by divine beings. So instead of forcing the gods to follow them, the Mesopotamians chose to create barriers that could deflect or neutralize any negative force aimed at them.

So far, only defensive and witchcraft types of Āšipūtu magick has been talked about in length, and this isn't without reason. The other two major forms of Mesoptamain magick, liminal and aggressive, aren't the most pleasant to talk about. In fact, the latter of the two could be considered as bad, if not worse, than witchcraft. Aggressive spells that were completely legal at times included spells meant to charm the king, which could be used to gain political favors; forcing someone to fall in love, either with you or a person you know; and, probably worst of all, forcing a runaway slave to return to their master (Schwemer, 2014a). While these spells were sometimes grouped with other methods of witchcraft, the fact of the matter is that, at times, these spells were entirely legal to cast (Schwemer, 2014a). Only witchcraft was seen as illegal, so these spells that bordered between the two forms of legality shows how wicked even legal spells could be.

As mentioned earlier, though, most of the information found about Āšipūtu comes from historical texts. There aren't many, if any, modern-day practitioners, so it is hard to study modern practices. However, due to the Mesopotamian civilizations being considered the earliest in history, popular media likes to portray magic from the region in a similar way to witchcraft. This mostly comes through the "evil texts" or "evil idols" of the Sumerians, which were actually a group of people that resided in Mesopotamia. The truth is, while Āšipūtu did have spells that could be considered dark magick, the Sumerians and other Mesopotamians had a complex magick structure that wasn't entirely harmful, much less demonic. Their magick is certainly a morally questionable one, but not as bad as the movies make it out to be.

Obeah and Vodou

For witches, it can be argued that their existence was challenged by the ill will of humanity. For the Obeah and Vodou practitioners, the ill will of humanity brought them into existence. This is not because the two were created to do ill to others. It is because the suffering endured by the founders of the two was conducted by a cruel hand: a cruel hand most people know as the slave trade.

During the seventeenth century, the European powers, wishing to exploit the islands in the Caribbean, engaged in an African slave trade that displaced thousands of native Africans away from their homes. While the cruelties of this trade shouldn't be downplayed whatsoever, the focus of this book is not to criticize an inherently malicious practice. Instead, this book focuses on the new ideas that formed from such unfavorable conditions. Throughout the Caribbean, Africans from various ethnic groups came together to form diverse ideas. In Trinidad, the imported slaves formed Shango or Trinidad Orisha. In Cuba, Santeria took root. In Haiti, Vodou, more popularly known as voodoo, was created. Throughout the Caribbean, Obeah also took shape.

While all of these beliefs were born out of shared hardship, to say they are the same would be a disservice. This is especially true if one compares Obeah to Vodou. While both practices deal with spirits and seek to help others in their daily life, there are very few similarities between the two. For starters, Obeah's origins are attributed to the Ashanti people, who actually had a reputation amongst the French and Spanish for being rebellious. The British were not as timid, forcefully displacing thousands to the West Indies. Vodou, on the other hand, originated by combining the beliefs of the Dahomean, Kongo, Yoruba, and various other ethnic groups that were forced by the French to move to Haiti (McAlister, n.d.).

Besides origin differences, Obeah and Vodou also differ in how it is practiced. Obeah is primarily done by individual practitioners, and the rituals and methods are passed down from master to apprentice. In fact, like an overabundance of fantasy wizards, Obeah men or women usually inherit this power through their ancestry, meaning these master and apprentice relationships are often within the same family tree. There is a method to become an Obeah outside of such families, but the vast number of practitioners come from Obeah families.

Vodou is vastly different in these regards. Vodou has a structure that makes it more of a religion compared to its Obeah counterpart. These structures are centered around communities called *sosyete*, with the average priest being called a *manbo* or *houngan*. Priests devoted to a certain *loa,* important spirits within Vodou, are instead called an *ounsis*, though they still aid the *houngans* and *manbos* in their practice. Underneath the *ounsis* are the *petite-caye,* who serve a similar role but aren't as devoted (*Vodou and Obeah*, 2022).

The two beliefs also have different practices. Obeah has two focuses: magick and herbalism. Vodou, on the other hand, focuses primarily on group rituals meant to aid the people involved. In both cases, Obeah and Vodou conduct their practice to improve their health, romantic attractiveness, luck, and chances to evade the law. The last one may seem like a malicious act until one remembers the historical context of both practices. Obeah and Vodou were originally practiced by black people being enslaved by white people. Due to this, the rights granted to the slaves were heavily restricted, so what counts as a "crime" for a black person during that time period was far wider than that for a white person.

Obeah was actually illegal for much of its existence due to colonial pressure. White colonists, fearing that Obeah would threaten their position, passed laws to restrict the practice. This made it so Obeah practitioners had to work in secret, cementing the tradition of fixing people's problems on an individual level. Vodou found a way to circumnavigate such discrimination from affecting them, though in doing so, it brought up a new problem. In an act of disguising their faith, the early *houngans* mixed their beliefs with Catholic symbolism. Over time, this disguise became part of Vodou, though to what extent is up for debate. Some Vodou practitioners claim they are Catholics with a different name, saying the Catholic saints are the same as Vodou's *loa*. At the same time, there are practitioners that still hold the idea that Catholic symbolism is just for appearances. Like many faiths, Vodou doesn't have a head committee that determines what is and what isn't Vodou. Because of it, it is hard to gauge how much Catholicism is part of Vodou.

As said before, the Obeah focus primarily on individual practice with those seeking aid going to an Obeah man or woman to conduct a ritual for them. The Obeah practitioners also serve a protective role, using their knowledge to help others protect themselves from malicious spirits called duppies. This was sometimes done through the use of a fetish, an inanimate object that was carried for protection against such spirits (*Obeah and Myal*, n.d.). While the Vodou have similar goals to Obeah, their methods are different. Namely, the Vodou ask the *loa* for aid through a variety of methods. More popular examples involve drums, dancing, and being possessed by the *loa*, who in turn offer omens and blessings to their followers. Other methods include *veves*, symbols drawn out through the use of cornmeal, and voodoo dolls, which are used to attract the *loa* (Beyer, 2018a). As mentioned in a previous section, kolossoi are similar to the popular conception of a voodoo doll because voodoo doll depictions in popular media are more akin to kolossoi than actual voodoo dolls.

It should be noted that both Obeah and Vodou have variations when it comes to their practice. Vodou alone has several different distinct branches, including "Rada, Daome, Ibo, Nago, Dereal, Manding, Petwo, and Kongo" (McAlister, n.d.). Some Vodou branches practice Obeah's family structure by having familial spirits (McAlister, n.d.). Others conduct animal sacrifices in order to appease the *loa* (Beyer, 2018a). Despite these differences, Obeah, Vodou, and other beliefs that grew from a cruel period of history in the Caribbean show that even in the darkest of times, humanity will find hope and ways to empower themselves.

Powwow

Powwow, or Braucherei in Deitsch, is a type of Germanic magick mostly practiced in Pennsylvania. This form of magick was brought over by Germanic immigrants and is still practiced to some degree in the modern-day.

It should be noted that this "powwow" shouldn't be confused with the Native American powwow, which is a gathering of several indigenous communities meant to strengthen bonds between them while expressing their cultural pride. The two are not associated in any way other than the fact the two are done in North America.

Powwow is an interesting practice because similar to Vodou, it uses Christian iconography. Unlike Vodou, however, Powwow practitioners never used such symbols to hide their practice. Instead, Powwow directly connects itself with Christianity, claiming the spells are empowered by the strength of God. This creates a weird duality as Powwow has practices that one could associate with witchcraft while at the same time being fully devoted to the religion that has historically persecuted similar crafts. Yet, despite this, practitioners see themselves as no different from other Christians. In fact, in order for one to actually practice Powwow, they have to be Christian in faith.

Due to the nature of the Christian faith promoting selflessness and humility, Powwow primarily has spells focused on healing or protection. Healing spells are usually conducted through invocations that are assisted by consecrated objects and herbal remedies (Wigington, 2019b). Protection spells usually come in the form of hexes and other sacred symbols associated with Christianity. While healing and protection spells are the primary spells associated with Powwow, there is one type of Powwow magick they consider to be dark magic. According to Professor David Kriebel, *The Sixth and Seventh Books of Moses* is a volume that contains Powwow magic. Yet, unlike other books, *The Sixth and Seventh Books of Moses* contain rituals that enable the summoning of spirits, a concept that most Powwow practitioners consider to be taboo (Kriebel, 2002).

Powwow literature isn't restricted to texts containing dark rituals, though. One of the most famous works was written by John George Homan in 1820 under the title *Pow-Wows: or, Long Lost Friend*. The text featured many usable rituals, remedies, and trinkets to aid Powwow doctors in their practice. More practices appear in Albertus Magnus's works, which sometimes illustrate more forms of Christian magick. Albertus Magnus himself was a German saint from the thirteenth century, spending much of his time writing books. However, these writers aren't the only teachers of Powwow. Traditionally, those who learned Powwow learned it from a practitioner of the opposite sex through the use of oral tradition and practice. Due to the multitude of healing and protection spells, most who learn the craft become "Powwow doctors," who in turn promise to help those in need and never accept money for their practice (Wigington, 2019b).

Just as times change, so does the adherence to religion. While tradition states that Powwow doctors shouldn't accept money, according to Professor Kriebel, that is no longer the case. "'Entrepreneurial' Powwowers," as Kriebel calls them, go against tradition and expect people to pay for their services (Kriebel, 2002). While the traditional practitioners still exist, these entrepreneurial Powwowers do show that tradition does fade away in time. Still, according to Kriebel, these entrepreneurial types only really ask for payment for what he calls Type II and Type III rituals. Type I rituals are described as having no more than two ritual components, a lack of verbal components, and target a single illness or issue that is not life-threatening (Kriebel, 2002). Anything more complex or larger in terms of scope would fall into either Type II or Type III spells, though Kriebel does remark that Type II rituals have a likelihood of being conducted for free.

While God is the main power in this magick system, there is also the presence of herbal remedies. These remedies aren't simply restricted to humans nor are they only for healing. For example, in one ritual, a mixture of "wormwood, asafetida, and other herbs" are mixed with salt and "soil from your stable" (Wigington, 2019b). Once the items are mixed together, the mixture would be buried in front of a stable where livestock resides, protecting its residents from disease and theft (Wigington, 2019b). If we go by Kriebel's type categorization method, this spell would probably fit into either Type II or Type III.

The previously mentioned also shows that, while God may be the one contributing power to the Powwow doctor, his name or other holy names don't need to be invoked in order for a ritual to take effect. However, the opposite is also true. There are some spells that ask for holy aid without the use of anything material. For example, a ritual that is intended to stop bleeding involves the caster saying, "This is the day on which the injury happened. Blood, thou must stop, until the Virgin Mary brings forth another son," three times in a row (Dugan, n.d.). Rituals similar to these would fit Kriebel's category of Type I rituals, which are considered to be too simple for an entrepreneurial Powwower to charge for money.

Like many groups in the past, the Germans who originally practiced Powwow moved to America due to religious persecution back in their home region around the 17th and 18th centuries (Wigington, 2019b). It is unclear if this religious persecution was aimed at the practice or not, as modern Germany, we know didn't exist at the time. Instead, the region was still subdivided into several kingdoms united in a confederate called the Holy Roman Empire. This makes understanding the cause of the exodus complicated due to the fact each kingdom within the confederate would have varying levels of religious tolerance. Due to this, the actual forerunners of Powwow came from several different religious backgrounds, including Lutherans, Amish, Mennonites, Anabaptists, and other Protestant groups (Wigington, 2019b). Due to these groups being primarily Protestant in nature, one could theorize that this exodus was due to that affiliation rather than their practice of Powwow, as many of the practices that would later be implemented into Powwow dated back to before the Protestant Reformation (Wigington, 2019b).

Once the Germanic community settled themselves in, not a lot of history on Powwow could be found. Since *Pow-Wows: or, Long Lost Friend* was published a century later, it seems accurate to say that no one really had a problem with the practice. However, there is one exception to that rule that brings forth a very ironic twist. According to Professor Kriebel, the modern-day "Conservative (Eastern) Mennonites" view Powwow as a "work of Satan" (Kriebel, 2002). While there is no clear indication of how old this viewpoint is, this hostility has been noted as a contributing factor to the decline of the Powwow practice. This has made finding traditional practitioners of Powwow rare, with Kriebel noting that "there is a perception within the culture area that powwowing is no longer practiced and less than half of the people I spoke with had even heard of it" (Kriebel, 2002).

Thus Powwow lives in an ironic state, where the magick practice that devotes itself to the Christian faith is in turn denounced by Christians calling it the work of Satan. It does, unfortunately, track with history. Perhaps in time, Powwow will have a revitalization and be recognized as an interesting system of magick, or perhaps it is doomed to fade away into history like many other lost magick arts. In either case, Powwow certainly was an interesting blend of two concepts usually opposed to one another, though the opposition was usually restricted to one party.

Satanism

While many of the other forms of magick here are very old, some are rather new. Similar to Wiccans, the modern Satanist is very different from previous groups that worshiped the religious figure. While there were plenty of groups that worshiped Satan, it was neither organized nor directly connected to witchcraft. The first official Satanic church was created during the 1960s through the works of writer Anton LaVey. The most famous of these works is *The Satanic Bible*, which forms the outlines of his beliefs as well as the central core of the magick practiced by modern-day Satanists.

To begin with, magick in Satanism is divided into two main categories: Lesser Magic, which is non-ritualistic in nature, and Greater Magic, which requires a ritual. Of the two, Lesser Magic is easier to pin down, as it is only divided into three additional groups: lust, nostalgia, and fear (Timon, 2016). Greater Magic on the other hand is connected to every form of "basic human emotion," which makes it more varied than Lesser Magic (Timon, 2016). Due to the emotion-centric source of Satanic magick, *The Satanic Bible* emphasizes the importance of letting one's emotions flow freely and honestly. In fact, LaVey argues that the caster needs to be honest with their own desires. If not, the spell will not work and may even backfire.

Despite popular depictions, most modern Satanists don't actually trace their power to demons, or even Satan himself. In fact, LaVey made it clear that Satan in this context is not actually a character at all, but instead a force of nature that can be drawn upon to aid a person in their day-to-day lives (Timon, 2016). This force is directly connected to human emotion, and it is through intense emotion that one can invoke the powers granted by it. This emotional state includes touching upon one's more animalistic side, as LaVey claims that acting more animalistic provides the same, if not more, power than animal sacrifices (Timon, 2016). This goes against cultural depictions of Satanists using animal or human sacrifices, both of which go against LaVey's claims that invoking magick is an internal, not external, activity.

That being said, Satanic magick isn't entirely internal. There are materials and phrases needed in order for spells to go off successfully, including symbols and incantations. These parts are just as important as one's emotional state, as the wrong words or symbols can result in negative consequences. Additionally, the caster needs to be confident during the entire casting process, including before and after the spell has been cast (Timon, 2016). If the Satanist believes the spell won't, isn't, or didn't work, then the spell will not be as strong as someone who has kept faith in themselves and the magick they invoke.

A unique factor of Satanic magick is the target of the spells. With other practices, spells could target spirits, aspects of nature, or fate itself. However, Satanic magick can only target one thing: people (Timon, 2016). This is not to say these spells are entirely malevolent or that such spells can't be used to gain other items, but Satanic magick can't target things such as negativity or weather conditions. The former could be targeted if the Satanist wishes to make a person less negative or close-minded, but a space that is perceived as negative cannot be cleansed through Satanic magick. This limited targeting means there are generally only two types of outcomes that come from spells: they either aid a person or harm a person.

Satanic spells drawing upon compassion and lust are associated with aiding a person and require both the caster and the receiver to believe in the spell for the best effect. Lust spells are meant to make intercourse more pleasurable for both parties involved, meaning they rely on the consent of everyone in order to work. Meanwhile, compassion spells are meant to generally aid a person in either health, success, or a different but similar condition. Satanists also practice spells literally called "destruction spells," which are meant to harm or destroy an individual. Ironically, the less the target believes the destruction spell is effective, the stronger the spell is (Timon, 2016). This means that those who take Satanic magic seriously, follower or not, are less likely to be hurt by a destruction ritual compared to someone who disregards magick entirely. Additionally, people who aren't focusing, such as when they are sleeping, daydreaming, or bored, are also more susceptible to Satanic magic (Timon, 2016).

The magick LaVey describes has a philosophy that is distinctly separate from any other magick practices. Namely, LaVey believes that using words such as "good" or "evil" to describe any type of magick is ridiculous, as such ideals are based on one's relative position to magick (Timon, 2016). This means that, to a Satanist, you can't really claim that someone is doing dark magick. LaVey also addresses stage magic, which is a rarity to see when talking about magick. Rarer still is that LaVey somewhat embraces the idea that stage magic does have a bit of magick to it, though he fully recognizes that not all stage magic uses it (Timon, 2016). While not fully embraced, the presence and even discussion of stage magic being valid are unorthodox when referencing older systems of magick, which would most likely claim that stage magic is just trickery.

However, while LaVey was a bit more accepting of other concepts of magic, *The Satanic Bible* also disagrees with many other forms. Namely, LaVey rejects the notion that ancient magick is useful or has any other secrets not already present in *The Satanic Bible* (Timon, 2016). Contemporary practices are still acceptable, but practices that are long since forgotten don't have any secret powers hidden away. This is due to his retelling of history with a Satanist lens, which does have some alterations. Firstly, LaVey claims that the majority of the victims accused during the witch trials weren't witches, but instead true witches prospered in areas away from heavily populated cities and towns (Timon, 2016). Additionally, he claims that his brand of Satanists didn't fit the profile of would-be witch hunters, even claiming that some people were Satanists but just didn't know (Timon, 2016). The biggest claim, and one that is a bit hard to swallow, is that Satanists have dominated the world and will continue to dominate the world, though they have and will brand themselves differently as time passes (Timon, 2016). He further emphasizes this by claiming a "New Satanic Age" had dawned due to the bickering on the other side of the theological argument (Timon, 2016). While this would prove ironic later on, it should be noted that Satanic magick was still a part of Satanic belief, which has declared itself a religion.

With *The Satanic Bible* published, LaVey crowned himself the first "Black Pope," a title that actually has been used several times before. However, in a very ironic turn, the Satanic church had already begun to divide itself into separate churches, some claiming to be older than LaVey's Church of Satan (History.com Editors, 2019). However, the biggest threat to Satanists wasn't internal disagreements, but external enemies. This came in the form of the 1980s Satanic Panic, a time where Christian fundamentalists claim that children were being abused during Satanic rituals and that Satanism itself encouraged its members to turn into murderers (History.com Editors, 2019). While it is true that Satanism does promote the belief that one "should feel free to pursue their own happiness," it also makes sure that their followers realize that they aren't immune to the consequences of said actions (Beyer, 2019a). On a personal level, LaVey denounced those who harmed children, did commit animal sacrifices, and even did the general illegal activity (Beyer, 2019a). These denouncements did little to ease the fears of the Christian fundamentalists, blaming multiple tragic and horrific things on Satanists with little or no proof of their involvement. However, even though the image of Satanists was dragged through the mud, those who actually became victims of this hysteria were often, similar to the witch trials of old, other Christians (History.com Editors, 2019).

The Church of Satan survived the Satanic Panic but would change soon after. LaVey died, and his death left a power gap that resulted in his partner, Blanche Barton, fighting against his children for control of the church (History.com Editors, 2019). While this changed little for the church, the true breaking point came from an author, Peter H. Gilmore, who was assigned by Barton to promote the church (History.com Editors, 2019). Gilmore claimed that the Church of Satan members were the only true Satanists, and this claim resulted in more Satanic branches forming, an event very reminiscent of the Protestant Reformation (History.com Editors, 2019).

Despite the many divisions, there are still notable Satanic churches. The Satanic Temple claims to be the new "primary religious Satanic organization in the world with congregations internationally," noting on their website that they disagree with the much older Church of Satan (*About Us*, n.d.). These differences do not stop the Satanic Temple from practicing magick, with their website providing rituals one can perform themselves. While it will most likely be a long time before they are painted in a positive light in the media, actual Satanists are just as varied as their Christian counterparts, having several different branches that can and will disagree on certain topics. However, looking into *The Satanic Bible* and LaVey's work shows a form of magick that is not only new but rather unique compared to older faiths.

Seiðr and Runes

Seiðr is a type of Norse magick or *fjölkynngi*.

Seiðr is primarily seen as divination magick, though some lump other abilities onto it. Culturally speaking, Seiðr is seen as something only women are supposed to do. Why this is isn't entirely clear, though evidence suggests that part of it was due to some rituals that involved weaving and the fact it originated from the goddess Freya. Women could become professional practitioners of Seiðr, earning the title of "völva" or "seiðkona." Men could technically practice the craft to become "seiðmaðr," but being a seiðmaðr was seen as a great shame as it was seen as unmanly in Norse society. Even in a mythological sense, Odin was berated by Loki for practicing Seiðr, the trickster god claiming that Odin was acting unmanly because of it.

Though the definition of Seiðr is a bit loose; the two major uses for this magick are to either find out what fate has for a person or to shift fate for the desired outcome. How these rituals were done is up to debate as there are no clear historical records on the traditional methods or at least official ones. However, there is a consensus that claims that "seiðr was a practice in which the magician used spinning to conjure spirits" (Storesund, 2017). The "spinning" involved was not of the bodily kind but of threads. In Norse mythology, a trio of goddesses called the Norns helped form the Web of Wyrd, extending threads that craft the fates of all life. Seiðr is meant to allow the caster to peer at the crafting of the Web of Wyrd and alter it if they so choose. Thus, in order to alter the tapestry of fate, the practitioner would need to weave their alteration into the web.

Seiðr was not the only magick practiced by the Norse, however. Another form is Spá or Spae, an art similar to Seiðr in the sense that both focus on investigating the fate and how things will play out. Unlike Seiðr, however, Spá merely looks at the Web of Wyrd instead of altering it. There is also Galdr, a music-based form of magick that came in either a song or chant. However, the most commonly referenced form of magick from this group comes in the form of rune magick.

To assume that Norse runes were strictly used for magickal purposes would be incorrect. The runes used for magick came from the actual alphabet for the Norse. Due to this, besides spells that only used runes, other forms of Norse magick, such as Spá and Galdr, also used these symbols for their rituals. Additionally, runes were used for communication and mundane tasks, so the mere presence of runes doesn't automatically indicate the application of magick. In fact, a common mistake for modern practitioners is not invoking the runes to activate their magickal properties after writing them down (Vamvoukakis, n.d.). Without invoking them, these runes just form a sentence, assuming the writer wrote the sentence correctly.

The spelling and order of the runes are very important when one is wishing to conduct a Norse rune magick. To explain it simply, how runes are arranged determines the meaning of the spell in a way similar to how the presence or absence of a comma alters an entire sentence. Just like how "Let's eat grandma" and "Let's eat, grandma" mean two different things, so too does a minor shifting of runes. A common story that is often pointed to illustrate this fact comes from the Saga of Egil Skallagrimsson.

Though the exact details are somewhat vague, the overall message and series of events are clear. One day, Egil Skallagrimsson was called to see an ill woman. Upon searching her bed, Egil found a set of runes that were making her sick. These runes weren't part of a malicious plot, however, but instead an act of an admirer who wanted to strengthen their relationship with the woman for one reason or another. Due to an incorrect arrangement of runes, this attempt at romanticizing turned deadly. Egil quickly made a new set of runes to replace the illness-causing set, resulting in the woman making a speedy recovery. This story not only details the importance of making sure you are writing the runes down in the correct order but also shows the potential harm that can be caused when they are improperly ordered.

However, merely understanding how the rune appears regularly isn't enough. There are other ways a rune can appear, and this alteration in appearance alters the meaning of the rune itself. For example, if a rune is inverted from its regular position, the original meaning becomes its opposite (Vamvoukakis, n.d.). So an inverted Raidho, which usually means road or journey, becomes a symbol meaning to stay in one place or a state of stagnation. There are also mirrored runes, which boost the strength of the rune at the cost of a slight alteration (Vamvoukakis, n.d.). A mirrored rune appears as the name suggests, which is to make the rune appear like it would in a mirror. Think of it like making a "b" look like "d". Due to the nature of some runes, they do not have a mirror, either because it is symmetrical or because their theoretical mirror rune becomes an entirely different and preexisting rune (Vamvoukakis, n.d.). So while all runes have an inverted rune, not all runes have a mirrored one.

The invocation of runes themselves does vary from spell to spell. As mentioned previously, rune stones can be used in a form of divination where the activation of the runes' predicting powers comes from simply posing a question. In a sense, that form of rune use aligns with the practice of Spá. However, while rune stones are one form in which runes could present themselves, it is not only one. In fact, there aren't really any historical rules about what medium runes have to be present in (Vamvoukakis, n.d.). The runes themselves do have to be legible, there is no denying that, but where these runes are placed is basically determined by the caster or carver. In fact, evidence suggests that there is some crossover between runic magick and how people regularly characterize fictional wizards. Among numerous medieval relics are staffs and wands with engraved runes on them, which were "waved at the person, who its user wished to 'catch'" the effects of the spell (*Runic Magic*, n.d.).

The Norse had a variety of magickal practices and tales associated with them, the actual art of conducting some of these rituals has been lost to time. We may never know the full extent of such magickal arts, which makes the information we have collected all the more valuable.

Thelema Magick

Thelema magick is interesting as it is another system that defines itself with the term "magick." One may assume that this is due to Thelema magick being younger than other forms discussed here. That assumption would be correct, as Thelema was first officially created in 1904 by a man named Aleister Crowley. Much of the magick described in Thelema relates back to the core of Crowley's beliefs that have become the Thelema faith. Due to this connection, it seems appropriate to examine the life of Crowley and how he eventually became the founder of a whole new belief system.

Aleister Crowley was born as Edward Alexander Crowley in 1875 in Royal Leamington Spa, England. While he was born in a Christian household, he grew up to dislike the faith. This would later influence Thelema, but Crowley chose to express his distaste in a much more personal way during his early life. He adopted the monicor "the Beast'" and aligned himself with the number 666. However, his more famous name change didn't occur until he started going to the University of Cambridge, where he finally adopted the name Aleister

Crowley.

After his time in college, he began traveling around the world in 1898. Crowley was very busy during his travels, writing a book of poetry and joining a group called the Hermetic Order of the Golden Dawn. His membership with the order was short-lived, leaving only two years later. However, the ceremonial practices of the Hermetic Order would later be incorporated into Thelema magick, as well as the yoga techniques Crowley learned during his travels (White, 2020). However, the most important event to occur during his travels was during his time in Egypt in the year 1904. During his time there, he claimed to have spoken to Horus, the Egyptian deity, who instructed him to write *The Book of Law*.

The Book of Law, or *Liber AL vel Legis*, would become the frame for the ideals expressed in the Thelema faith. However, it was not his only book relating to Thelema. In fact, in 1929, he wrote *Magick*, a book that was aimed at explaining the true nature of magick within the Thelema system. This includes a clear definition for magick in this context as Crowley writes, "MAGICK is the Science and Art of causing Change to occur in conformity with Will" (Crowley, 1929). "Will" in this context relates back to the base belief of Thelema.

Thelema works on the principle that everyone has a "True Will." In fact, Thelema means "will" in Greek. This "True Will" is akin to destiny, though unlike the pure concept of destiny, a person could theoretically never reach their True Will. In order to even understand if one is on the right path to discover their True Will, a person needs to find their unique traits and qualities to discover their "True Self" (Beyer, 2019b). Not discovering one's True Self isn't entirely bad, as people could accidentally follow their True Will without realizing it. However, according to Crowley, misery and a lack of productivity is caused by a person going against their True Will, such as "a boy's instinct may tell him to go to sea, while his parents insist on his becoming a doctor. In such a case, he will be both unsuccessful and unhappy in medicine" (Crowley, 1929). Since misery is caused by going against one's True Will, following one's True Will results in happiness and the best results from a person's abilities.

Now, this does raise a concern. Supposedly, what if a True Will of one contradicts the True Will of another? According to Crowley, "Every man has a right to fulfill his own will without being afraid that it may interfere with that of others; for if he is in his proper place, it is the fault of others if they interfere with him" (Crowley, 1929). While this quote isn't directly related to that question, it does help answer it if we looked beyond the individual. If a group of people follow Crowley's teachings and commit to their True Will, according to this statement, no one within that group should be "interfering" with others members. If there is, then it was that individual's choice to cause harm or inconvenience to another person. This means that, while True Wills may be different from person to person, the accomplishment of one's True Will shouldn't block another person from achieving their True Will.

One might rightfully ask what any of this has to do with Thelema magick. The simple answer is that Thelema magick is different from other forms of magick when it comes to purpose. When observing the other kinds, one can get a general theme: magick is used to help a person gain something through the use of ritual. Sometimes these magick systems have no ties with destiny, and other times, they directly influence the flow of destiny. Magick in Thelema is solely used to help achieve one's destiny, or in this case, True Will. This minor difference means a person needs to be very self-aware about their wants and desires, as going against one's True Will with magick results in the same consequence as going against one's True Will in every other situation: misery and a lack of productivity.

There are other things that separate Thelema magick from other types. Firstly, Crowley claims that "Every intentional act is a Magical Act" (Crowley, 1929). While there are certain rituals in Thelema magick, akin to Kotodama with their ever-present power of certain words, every action intentionally conducted is considered to hold magick power for followers of Thelema. This concept doesn't stray too far from the definition Crowley used to explain Thelema magick where it is used to align the person and world closer to one's True Will. Since every action has consequences, using actions to get closer to one's Will would make such actions magickal in nature. However, seeing how one can conduct actions that can result in going against one's True Will, it can be assumed that magick conducted can both help and harm the caster in this context.

Thelema magick, while still being relatively new in terms of magick systems, does inherit a trait most commonly found in older forms of magick and religion. Thelema magick incorporates science into its overall structure, with text supporting an alchemic flair to Crowley's views on the subject. Crowley does admit that "we cannot cause eclipses, for instance, or transform lead into the tin, or create men from mushrooms," though he does say that "it is theoretically possible to cause in any object any change of which that object is capable by nature" (Crowley, 1929). The only thing preventing us from doing the things he admits we cannot do is, according to him, the knowledge and power we currently lack.

As noted previously, two major influences on magick rituals in the Thelema faith are rituals conducted by the Hermetic Order of the Golden Dawn and yoga practices. These rituals may not be totally separate from everyday actions in terms of purpose, but they are designed to better strengthen a person's perception of their personal True Will. However, Crowley did experiment with a type of magick that could be seen as controversial by several.

In 1912, Crowley became head of the Ordo Templi Orientis (OTO), a fraternity overseen by a German socialist by the name of Theodor Reuss (White, 2020). The fraternity sought to unify all Masonic and Hermetic systems into one connected system. This includes a type of magic that Crowley began experimenting with in the year 1914: sexual magick (White, 2020). As sexual magick is a very complex topic that requires a lot of nuances, this book will not be going into that subject matter. The necessity of mentioning it in the first place is to show that Crowley's life was not free of controversy. In fact, one could say it was plagued by it.

In 1905, while traveling up Kanchenjunga, one of the largest mountains in the world, Crowley's group encountered an avalanche. Some claim that Crowley ignored the cries of his fellow expedition members as they struggled against the cold and snow (The Editors of Encyclopaedia Britannica, 2021). Additionally, in 1923, a young man died in Sicily after supposedly doing Thelemic rituals. This event would later result in Crowley being forced out of Italy, with the OTO branch in the region slowly drifting away into obscurity (White, 2020). However, OTO is still around today and is considered the largest Thelemic organization, consisting of about 4,000 members (White, 2020).

While Crowley's life could be seen as morally gray, the system of magick he created is unique in several aspects. Additionally, researchers have contributed great power to Crowley's work and philosophy. Some claim that Crowley helped jump-start many of the newer magick faiths that would develop, while others examine how Crowley's individualistic philosophy influenced society. If you wish to explore and maybe even practice Thelema magick, remember that even though Thelema magick is focused on an individual's unique True Will, your True Will shouldn't prevent people from engaging with their own True Will.

Wuism

Also referred to as Chinese shamanism, Wuism is not one unified set of spells or rituals, but instead an umbrella term to refer to several similar forms of magick conducted by the several ethnic groups that are now part of present-day China. While still practiced today to some extent, Wuism is unique due to its history. Similar to witchcraft in Europe, practitioners of Wuism were discriminated against, but at the same time, some practitioners were venerated. This paradoxical nature has a direct relationship with Chinese centralization.

In the very beginning of Wuism, both males and females were considered able to conduct the practice. While certain documents differentiate the practitioners by sex, calling men practitioners *xi* or shamans and women as *wu* or shamanesses, it is more common that practitioners were simply referred to as *wu*. Similar to many fictional depictions of magic, not everyone can become a *wu*. According to archaeologist Tong Enzheng, "the ancient *wu* was unusual from birth. Whether they were possessed by supernatural beings or embarked on a spiritual journey, *wu* needed to be preternaturally sensitive in their emotions" (Enzheng, 2002). Despite this unusualness, the *wu* wasn't discriminated against at this time. They were instead seen as an important member of their family and their community, using their power to predict fortunes and misfortunes that members of their village would encounter (Enzheng, 2002). A thing to note was that this ability wasn't seen as a full occupation, simply an additional responsibility a *wu* had in order to support their community.

Then China began to centralize. The *wu*'s unique position allowed them to obtain higher status becoming part of the elite class (Enzheng, 2002). This rise also gave rise to emperors claiming to be *wu*. Amongst these was the Yellow Emperor who claimed to have the ability to speak to spirits and Emperor Shun who was said to have perfect navigational abilities (Enzheng, 2002). Along with the classification's increased prestige, the roles and responsibilities of the *wu* changed. Alongside their previous responsibilities as *wu*, the practitioners became judges, writers, calendric and astrological observers, doctors, and record keepers (Enzheng, 2002).

Despite this rise in power, *wu*'s position wasn't always a kind one. During the rule of Tang of the Shang Dynasty, a story claims that Tang himself suffered and prayed for forgiveness during a drought that devastated the land. The gods, feeling pity, sent down hard rain that countered the devastation caused by the drought. This act inspired similar rituals where *wu* would be bound, nude, and exposed to the elements in order to invoke divine pity and rain (Enzheng, 2002). Alongside potentially deadly rituals, the political power of *wu* began to dissipate, with the earliest period of this decline happening during the Western Zhou dynasty, which started around 1050 B.C. (Enzheng, 2002). However, even with decreased power, *wu* were still used for their divination abilities, though the divinations that were being asked for now focused more on the state instead of a single community or family.

Despite many *wu* being in higher positions of power, there were still records of *wu* on a local level that conduct much of the same rituals conducted by their earlier incarnations.

However, even though local *wu* was conducting historical practices that many were fine with for decades, they were discriminated against by the Chinese government in this new age. This came from a differentiation in the practices conducted between the elite, sanctioned *wu,* and the local *wu*. Those *wu* in positions of authority claimed to have their power tied to divine deities and spirits. In contrast, the local *wu* still cited their visions as coming from the aid of spirits that weren't technically gods or goddesses. This division in faith created a divide between the two types of *wu*, resulting in discrimination that disproportionately harmed those who stuck with the old faith. Thus, practitioners of Wuism were both discriminated against and venerated.

Beyond history, Wuism is different from much of the magick discussed in this book. While rituals make up the bulk of the practice, these rituals are different as they are primarily conducted through music and dance. The exact procedure of the spell depended on the practitioner's background and placement in society as local *wu* usually conducted the dance by themselves, unlike their more structured counterparts in the government who practiced in groups. However, one unifying factor that seems present in the majority of rituals were drums. Archaeologist Enzheng noted that in many recorded rituals, "the drum was the most significant instrument," even during wartime. This was because, even before a battle, drums "were still associated with magical dancing" and were used "to boost the fighting spirit of one's own side and to threaten the enemy" (Enzheng, 2002). The combination of music and dance in order to cast spells is an uncommon concept, even in fictional stories where they use the former without the latter.

In addition to these practices, a subgroup of *wu* emerged called the *fangshi*, which can translate to "recipe master." While they were still considered *wu*, the *fangshi* were strictly part of the elites who worked for the Chinese government. While they conducted the duty excepted by every *wu* practitioner of their time, they are most famous for their potion-making. Specifically, they are famous for their research into an elixir of immortality. They were more than that, though, being what many would consider being scientists nowadays, with them conducting experiments to see what happens when compounds are mixed together.

Wuism today is still a bit of a touchy subject for China. During the development of the First Republic of China, certain branches of Wuism were forbidden and the elite *wu* practitioners lost their post (Naef-Tahvanainen, 2014). However, as recently as 2014, this perspective has begun to change alongside China's efforts to reintroduce and praise China's historical culture, though the practice does have some new governmental influence (Naef-Tahvanainen, 2014). Even if it gets rejected again in the future, Wuism will most likely endure as it had for centuries.

Chaos Magic

Chaos magic is not an actual system of magick, and yet, at the same time, it is. If one recalls all the way back in Chapter 1, eclectic witches are a type of witch that incorporates several practices into a singular, personal practice. Chaos magic works the same way with one minor difference: there is no personal practice. Sure, someone practicing Chaos magic can use the same rituals over and over again, but they don't *have* to. Chaos magic focuses on the here and now. Any rituals conducted by a Chaos magician are done because the magician themselves think it will work for a specific time and place. If the next day they wish to conduct another spell in order to get the same effect, the Chaos magic practitioner can reject the old spell and conduct a new one. The second spell doesn't invalidate the first, for, at both times, the practitioner believes the spells will work.

"How does this make any sense?" one could ask themselves. It is a very valid question. All the previous magick systems, even if they have divergences between groups who claim the same practice, have some level of consistency. While Chaos magicians may disagree on the exact specifics of the source of magick in this context, the general idea is that magick is something invoked by the person, not the actions directly. Chaos magicians see rituals as a method to get into the proper state of mind that enables them to perform magick, but the ritual itself is overall meaningless. The caster's intentions have more power than the performance they conduct.

Compared to the other forms of magick, Chaos magic is an outlier when it comes to freedom of practice as there is no concrete way to describe the practice. That being said, while the practice itself is chaotic, the history behind it is not. While it would be appropriate for Chaos magic to be thought up by several individuals all at the same time, in an ironic twist, most people associated the formation of Chaos magic with one writer: Austin Osman Spare.

Austin Osman Spare was born in December

1886 in London, England. At an early age, Spare had a talent for art, a talent of his that he used to his fullest. In 1904, despite being only in his teens, his work was accepted into the Royal College of Arts summer exhibition, solidifying his career as an artist for a brief period of time, but time passed and his favor with critics slowly died out. It was around this time that Spare began to investigate magick practices. This investigation eventually led Austin Spare to meet a key occultist figure of the time: Aleister Crowley.

At first, Spare and Crowley were friendly toward one another. However, as Spare looked further into the structured faith organized by Crowley, the more hostile the two became towards each other. Spare began to outwardly criticize the ceremonial practices that "prevented the practitioner from discovering his/her own power" (*Chaos Magick*, 2022). Desiring to make an alternative, Spare created a sigil form of magick that was designed to be easier than Crowley's Thelemic rituals. In truth, while Spare did create the base of what would eventually be Chaos magic, Spare never actually called what he did "chaos magic," nor was his sigil magick a prototype for said practice (Beyer, 2018b). However, his criticisms would eventually inspire other writers to challenge ceremonial practices that would lead to the formation of Chaos magic.

Ray Sherwin and Peter J. Carroll are two such writers. The two published works around the same time, making it hard to determine who was the more influential of the two. Sherwin mostly wrote works promoting Chaos Magic, including *The Book of Results* in 1983 and *The Theatre of Magick* in 1989 (*Chaos Magick*, 2022). In contrast, Carroll helped create several Chaos magician covens during the 1970s and 1980s (Beyer, 2018b). Carroll did write after Sherwin's works were published, with *Psychonaut* being one where Carroll covers the theory and practice of Chaos magic (*Chaos Magick*, 2022). While one could argue over who was the larger contributor to the practice, no one can deny that the two at least contributed to the spread and continuation of Chaos magic practices.

The most fascinating aspect of Chaos magic is the fact that everything in this book could theoretically be used for this system of magick. While the rituals themselves are meaningless to a Chaos magician, the act of conducting them enables their magick to prosper. While they might not adopt the significance of earlier chapters, they may mimic the motions in order to conduct their own spells. The same couldn't be said for other casters in this text, as some practices conducted by one type conflict or avoid practices done by another group. In an ironic sense, Chaos magicians might be one of the most unifying of all; unified in a practice of inconsistency.

CONCLUSION

Media likes to portray magic as this earth-shattering thing that could rip the world apart if placed into the hands of evil people. Real magick is neither that grandiose nor that powerful. However, throughout the ages, people around the world have found it reliable in one form or another. From the witches, both modern and old, who use magick to cast spells, to the astrologists and numerologists who examine the world through observations, and to the druids and other practitioners who tap into ancient practices, magick has been used to make predictions and to alter the world in much more subtle ways.

This book went over the complex history many of these systems have as well as some of the beliefs around them. Materials used for spells were analyzed to see what their purpose is and how one may apply them to one's own rituals. This guide went over how to prepare for a spell and how to conduct it, including how one can make their own magic circle. This book helped show a process about how one can make their very own spells if they so choose. Finally, this book explored alternative forms of magick that have their own systems, many connected to a complex philosophy and history that separates them from their peers.

To those young spellcasters wishing to conduct their first rituals, congratulations. This is by no means a fully detailed book going over everything about spells, but this should be more than enough to get you started on your first spells. Just remember that spells aren't going to fix all your problems. They can help alleviate some of the work, but you still have to put in the effort in your day-to-day life. The less a spell has to change, the more likely it will succeed.

To the more skeptical among you, your misgivings on accepting the validity of magick are perfectly fine. This book was by no means an argument about the truthfulness of the practice, merely a guide to it. Hopefully, you've learned something from this text. Perhaps you discovered the truly complex nature of witchcraft. Perhaps you found the history surrounding the different magick practitioners interesting and wish to learn more about a group's history. Maybe this book has piqued your interest in exploring other topics related to magick, even if you don't believe in it. Whatever it is, I hope you find some joy in reading this book. Who knows? Perhaps you might try making a spell one day.

SUBSCRIBE TO SOFIA VISCONTI

Greetings!

As a subscriber, you will receive a **Free Gift** + you will be the first to hear about new books, articles and more exclusives **just for you.**

Simply scan the qr code to join.

References

About us. (n.d.). The Satanic Temple. https://thesatanictemple.com/pages/about-us

Ár nDraíocht Féin – our own druidry. (2022). Ár nDraíocht Féin. https://staging.ng.adf.org/

Beyer, C. (2018a, May 2). *An introduction to the basic beliefs of the vodou (voodoo) religion*. Learn Religions. https://www.learnreligions.com/vodou-an-introduction-for-beginners-95712

Beyer, C. (2018b, August 13). *What is chaos magic?* Learn Religions. https://www.learnreligions.com/chaos-magic-95940

Beyer, C. (2019a, January 26). *LaVeyan satanism and the church of satan*. Learn Religions. https://www.learnreligions.com/laveyan-satanism-church-of-satan-95697

Beyer, C. (2019b, January 27). *Understanding the religion of thelema*. Learn Religions. https://www.learnreligions.com/thelema-95700

Chaos magick. (2022, August 2). Encyclopedia.com. https://www.encyclopedia.com/science/encyclopedias-almanacs-transcripts-and-maps/chaos-magick

Connolly, S.B. (2016, June 11). *Bamberg, Germany: The early modern witch burning stronghold*. History... The Interesting Bits! https://historytheinterestingbits.com/2016/06/11/bamberg-germany-the-early-modern-witch-burning-stronghold/

Crowley, A. (1929). *Introduction to magick*. Weiser Books. Thelema 101. https://www.thelema101.com/magick-i

Dugan, P.J. (n.d.). *The origin and practition of pow-wow*. Berks History Center. https://www.berkshistory.org/multimedia/articles/pow-wow/

Enzheng, T. (2002, January 1). Magicians, magic, and shamanism in ancient China. *Journal of East Asian*

Archaeology, *4*(1), 27–73. https://doi.org/10.1163/156852302322454495

Forest, D. (2020, November 30). *Wild magic: Simple ways to step into celtic folk magick*. Llewellyn Worldwide. https://www.llewellyn.com/journal/article/2858

Gardner, Gerald Brousseau. (n.d.). World Religions Reference Library; Encyclopedia.com. https://www.encyclopedia.com/religion/encyclopedias-almanacs-transcripts-and-maps/gardner-gerald-brousseau

Geeraert, A. (2020, August 3). *Kotodama: The spiritual power of words in Japanese culture*. Kokoro Media. https://kokoro-jp.com/culture/1147/

Goêteia explorations in chthonic sorcery. (n.d.). Theomagica. https://theomagica.com/goeteia

Hayward, L. (2020, March 11). *Magic in ancient Greece and rome*. TheCollector. https://www.thecollector.com/magic-in-ancient-greece-and-rome/

Healing and medicine: Healing and medicine in the ancient near east. (2022, June 22). Encyclopedia.com. https://www.encyclopedia.com/environment/encyclopedias-almanacs-transcripts-and-maps/healing-and-medicine-healing-and-medicine-ancient-near-east

History.com Editors. (2017, September 12). *History of witches*. History; A&E Television Networks. https://www.history.com/topics/folklore/history-of-witches

History.com Editors. (2018a, April 6). *Samhain*. History; A&E Television Networks. https://www.history.com/topics/holidays/samhain

History.com Editors. (2018b, March 23). *Wicca*. History; A&E Television Networks. https://www.history.com/topics/religion/wicca

History.com Editors. (2019, September 27). *Satanism*. History; A&E Television Networks.

https://www.history.com/topics/1960s/satanism#anton-lavey

Hosokawa, N. (2014, May 24). *Kotodama: The multi-faced Japanese myth of the spirit of language*. OUPblog. https://blog.oup.com/2014/05/kotodama-japanese-spirit-of-language/

Kriebel, D.W. (2002). *Powwowing: A persistent american esoteric tradition*. Esoterica. http://esoteric.msu.edu/VolumeIV/Powwow.htm

Lewis, I.M., & Russell, J.B. (n.d.). *Witchcraft*. Encyclopædia Britannica. https://www.britannica.com/topic/witchcraft

Maccrossan, T. (2002, May 29). *Celtic magic*. Llewellyn Worldwide. https://www.llewellyn.com/encyclopedia/article/193

McAlister, E.A. (n.d.). *Vodou*. Encyclopædia Britannica. https://www.britannica.com/topic/Vodou

Mirelman, S. (2018, August 21). Mesopotamian magic in text and performance. *Mesopotamian Medicine and Magic, 14,* 343–378. https://doi.org/10.1163/9789004368088_018

Naef-Tahvanainen, K. (2014, August 5). *Popular religious practices in China: Shamanism or "wuism."* Life in China Today. https://lifeinchinatoday.com/tag/wuism/

Obeah and myal. (n.d.). Vcu.edu. http://www.people.vcu.edu/~wchan/poco/624/harris_south/Obeah%20and%20Myal.htm

Our courses and membership. (n.d.). Order of Bards, Ovates & Druids. https://druidry.org/our-courses

Pinch, G. (2011, February 17). *Ancient egyptian magic*. Www.bbc.co.uk. https://www.bbc.co.uk/history/ancient/egyptians/magic_01.shtml

Purkiss, D. (n.d.). *A journey into witchcraft beliefs*. English Heritage. https://www.english-heritage.org.uk/learn/histories/journey-into-witchcraft-beliefs/

Runic magic. (n.d.). National Museum of Denmark. https://en.natmus.dk/historical-knowledge/denmark/prehistoric-period-until-1050-ad/the-viking-age/religion-magic-death-and-rituals/runic-magic/

Said, M. (2018, December). *Mesopotamian magic in the first millennium b.c.* Metmuseum.org; The Metropolitan Museum of Art. https://www.metmuseum.org/toah/hd/magic/hd_magic.htm

Schwemer, D. (2014a, September). *Witchcraft in ancient mesopotamia.* American Society of Overseas Research (ASOR). https://www.asor.org/anetoday/2014/09/witchcraft-in-ancient-mesopotamia/

Schwemer, D. (2014b). *Mesopotamian magic.* Universität Würzburg. https://www.phil.uni-wuerzburg.de/cmawro/magic-witchcraft/mesopotamian-magic/

Storesund, E. (2017, May 1). *Sex, drugs, and drop-spindles: What is seiðr? (Norse metaphysics pt. 2).* Brute Norse. https://www.brutenorse.com/blog/2017/05/sex-drugs-and-drop-spindles-what-is.html

The Editors of Encyclopaedia Britannica. (2021, November 27). *Aleister Crowley.* Encyclopædia Britannica. https://www.britannica.com/biography/Aleister-Crowley

Timon, C.E. (2016, July 22). What is magic to the LaVeyan-satanist ideal type?: A content-analysis of the satanic bible's descriptions of magic. *Anthropology Summer Fellows, 1.* https://digitalcommons.ursinus.edu/cgi/viewcontent.cgi?article=1000&context=anth_sum

Vamvoukakis, A. (n.d.). *Runic magic – history and practice.* The Embroidered Forest. https://theembroideredforest.com/blogs/magic/run

ic-magic

Vodou and obeah. (2022, August 26). Gale Library of Daily Life: Slavery in America; Encyclopedia.com. https://www.encyclopedia.com/humanities/applied-and-social-sciences-magazines/vodou-and-obeah

White, M.H. (2020, December 14). Rethinking Aleister Crowley and thelema. *Aries*, *21*(1), 1–11. https://doi.org/10.1163/15700593-02101004

Wigington, P. (2019a, May 13). *Biography of Gerald Gardner and the gardnerian wiccan tradition*. Learn Religions. https://www.learnreligions.com/what-is-gardnerian-wicca-2562910

Wigington, P. (2019b, December 28). *Folk magic powwow: History and practices*. Learn Religions. https://www.learnreligions.com/powwow-folk-magic-4779937

Other Books By Sofia Visconti

Available now in Ebook, Paperback, Hardcover, and Audiobook in all regions.

THE BOOK OF SPELLS FOR BEGINNERS

We sincerely hope you enjoyed our new book **"The Book of Spells for Beginners"**. We would greatly appreciate your feedback with an honest review at the place of purchase.

First and foremost, we are always looking to grow and improve as a team. It is reassuring to hear what works, as well as receive constructive feedback on what should improve. Second, starting out as an unknown author is exceedingly difficult, and Amazon reviews go a long way toward making the journey out of anonymity possible. Please take a few minutes to write an honest review.

Best regards,

Sofia Visconti